BALLOON

Karen Sunde

BROADWAY PLAY PUBLISHING INC
New York
www.broadwayplaypublishing.com
info@broadwayplaypublishing.com

BALLOON
© Copyright 1983 Karen Sunde

All rights reserved. This work is fully protected under the copyright laws of the United States of America. No part of this publication may be photocopied, reproduced, stored in a retrieval system, or transmitted, in any form or by any means, electronic, mechanical, recording, or otherwise, without the prior permission of the publisher. Additional copies of this play are available from the publisher.

Written permission is required for live performance of any sort. This includes readings, cuttings, scenes, and excerpts. For amateur and stock performances, please contact Broadway Play Publishing Inc. For all other rights please contact the author c/o B P P I.

Cover art by Rick Butler

First edition: March 1983
This edition: October 2017
I S B N: 978-0-88145-006-4

Book design: Marie Donovan
Page make-up: Adobe InDesign
Typefaces: Palatino & Baskerville set by BakerSmith Type, N Y C

SETTING:

The Salon of Madame Helvetius, about 1784.

A small round table with haphazard array of flowers in a basket, and 5-7 lightweight chairs in any arrangement are sufficient. The room is a solarium leading to the garden.

CHARACTERS:

HELVETIUS, Anne-Catherine
MORELLET, writer, scientist
TURGOT, former Minister of Finance for Louis XVI
ROCHE, scholar
CABANIS, disciple of Turgot
FRANKLIN, Benjamin—affectionately "Papa"

> FRANKLIN is the old man here, CABANIS the young. The rest are middle-age contemporaries with HELVETIUS balancing towards FRANKLIN.

> Other characters appear, but only as created during the 'charades' of the evening:
> HELVETIUS plays POLLY STEVENSON and MISS HOWE, MORELLET plays ADMIRAL HOWE and BEAUMARCHAIS, TURGOT plays WEDDERBURN and CHAUMONT, CABANIS plays WILLIAM FRANKLIN and LOUIS XVI

If you were to walk in unseen on these friends they would all be speaking, out of turn, about whatever concerned each most at that instant, but if you stayed through the first drink you would soon know them, and see why their life together, straddling three worlds and two revolutions, was so exciting.

BALLOON—Notes:

The play takes place on the eve of Franklin's departure from France, in the Salon of a woman he does not want to leave. His friends, literary, scientific and political figures, prevail on him to re-enact scenes from his past life, and a play-within-a-play develops.

The characters are by turns excited and disturbed by the scenes they enact; one scene begins to demand the next; characters begin to identify or confuse themselves with what they play, and their present relationships are overwhelmed by what their playing reveals.

It begins like a parlor game, or in the mood of children at play: "Let's pretend I'm so-and-so, and you're so-and-so, and we do such-and-such." Or perhaps, even more precisely, it is like actors improvising: Two characters begin; the others watch and comment. A character "playing" may step out of his "scene" and speak to characters watching. Other characters may be moved to join, or to initiate their own scenes. Sometimes they are all drawn in to create a crowd.

Physically, it works very simply. First, the five or seven chairs are fluid: they may be moved anywhere by anyone. (This kaleidoscoping of the chairs, carefully choreographed, is very beautiful.) The characters use whatever they feel they need to create a scene. One scene calls for a table, two chairs, and a chess set, so the characters clear the table they have and use it. Those watching arrange themselves, a little apart, as spectators. A manuscript introduced in the beginning as a translation of Roche's is used more than once later as a prop by his friends. Two chairs become a carriage. No special acting area needs to be marked out; it will be spontaneously created by the needs of each scene. When the scenes swell to include all the characters, the whole room is their stage.

Act One

Thunder. Singing begins offstage. Enter, in loose garments, an easy, stately woman. She is singing a Scottish ballad, but she is French, and has difficulty getting it right. When she stumbles she laughs softly and tries again.

HELVETIUS: Last May a fine wooer came down the long glen,
And sore with his love he did tease me.
I said there was nothing I hated like men;
The deuce went with him to believe me, believe me.
The deuce went with him to believe me.

He spoke o' the darts o' my bonnie black eyes,
And vowed for my love he was dyin'.
I said he might die when he liked for his sighs;
The god-sakes forgive me for lyin', for lyin'.
The god-sakes forgive me for lyin'.

Before the end of the second stanza, she has crossed the stage, opened an umbrella, and gone off into the garden. As her singing fades we hear excited chatter.

MORELLET: *(Offstage.)* You'll see, you'll see, you'll see. Just come along.

ROCHE: *(Off.)* So they made it! Did they make it, Morellet?

TURGOT: *(Off.)* How many people were there?

ROCHE: *(Off.)* How long was it . . .

CABANIS: *(Off.)* How high did they get . . .

Group bursts on. MORELLET *at center with huge package.* ROCHE, TURGOT, *and* CABANIS *jostling attendance.*

MORELLET: There were thousands! At least ten thousand.

CABANIS: No getting through at all, I know. Here. Put it here.

CABANIS *moves basket of flowers from table to floor.* MORELLET *puts package in center of table. Others crowd around.*

ROCHE: But Morellet, you've been out there three nights! And days.

MORELLET: My God, you think I don't know. The excitement was incredible.

MORELLET *rests his arms on the package, envisioning scene.*

CABANIS: They had no idea when . . . no one could tell for sure when it would happen.

TURGOT: The package, Morellet?

MORELLET: Oh. Yes, yes yes . . . *(He begins to unwrap it, tantalizingly.)*

ROCHE: Where could you sleep?

MORELLET: Who knows.

ROCHE: Your cloak reeks.

MORELLET: You should have stayed, Roche. Dirtied your cloak in the bubbling street.

ROCHE: Is it true that even ladies . . .

MORELLET: But of course, my dear la Roche—everyone. Toute le monde. The ladies were brave enough to forego their toilettes, their sleep, their . . . amusements. Voila!

He has uncovered a ridiculous looking contraption: A model of the balloon. It is elliptical or sausage-shaped. The basket resembles a boat with oars extended, and a rudder. The whole is elaborately draped

Act One

and gilded like a wedding cake, only in bright colors. They are awestruck. CABANIS *may go on one knee in front of the table.*

MORELLET: *(Pause.)* An exact replica.

ROCHE: To be present at such a moment.

MORELLET: *(Pause.)* Yes.

ROCHE *brings a chair to the table, sits. Silence. All gazing at the balloon.*

TURGOT: It's not round.

MORELLET: No. The cylinder presents less surface to the air. Lowers resistance.

CABANIS: Where is the fire placed.

TURGOT: No fire. The air isn't hot. Oil of vitriole poured on iron shavings produces it.

MORELLET: A bird at dawn. She lifted so lightly.

ROCHE: What are these . . . wings?

MORELLET: Oars.

ROCHE: Oars?

TURGOT: *(Laughing.)* By god. Then that's a rudder.

MORELLET: Exactly.

TURGOT: *(Still laughing.)* Mon Dieu. Did it work?

MORELLET: Beauty, lightness, elegance. Look at the magnificent pavillion. Yes, like magic. It lifted on command. Rose, disappeared into the fog, as surely, as rapidly, as if it were the hundredth voyage.

All are intent on balloon. FRANKLIN *is entering. He is looking for someone, and will be in and out often.*

TURGOT: But did the wings—the oars—work.

FRANKLIN: *(Startles them from behind.)* They ripped it open. Took fright, poor fools. Afraid it would burst, they said, afraid they couldn't get down. They rose into storm, and ripped a hole in their balloon. Where is she?

ROCHE: My god. Did they fall?

FRANKLIN: Not quite. Came down faster than they should have. Almost landed in a pond. Terrified a woman out after her cows. Where is she? Silly chattering when I've had no taste of her. Has she been here?

TURGOT: Easy Papa. Let her be.

FRANKLIN: You know, they said that at the moment the fabric was punctured they could see neither earth nor sky. *(As he exits to the garden.)* But then they fell, and the earth came to meet them quick enough.

TURGOT *trails upstage looking after* FRANKLIN. *Others have gone back to studying balloon.*

TURGOT: There were a lot of people?

MORELLET: Thousands! Never, since the bread riots . . .

TURGOT: Didn't you hear rumbling.

MORELLET: Rumbling?

TURGOT: *(He moves back to balloon indicating decoration.)* That so many thousands of livres, so much magnificence should be expended on something so frivolous. What need was there for all this tapestry and gilding?

MORELLET: Ah, ah, ah, my dear Turgot. When did magnificence ever serve a need. It serves the spirit. All these people, from beggar to comtesse, were seized with the spirit of the thing. The peasant wasn't huddled in today's shivering dawn to protest twelve sous to the pound of bread. For the moment of this gathering he forgot bread altogether and stood dazzled—merely dazzled— by man's possibility.

ACT ONE

FRANKLIN *enters from garden.*

ROCHE: Aeronauts floating the skies. It's like a child's dream. But . . . what's the good of it. How can we use it.

FRANKLIN: What's the good of a new-born baby? *(Pause.)* She's been in the greenhouse, I know, *(touching the flowers)* and these are fresh . . .

ROCHE: Not fair, not a fair answer, Papa. All your experiments are practical. I'm the only dreamer in Madame's library.

FRANKLIN: Practical? Ah, my dear Roche, you are deceived. Victim of a vicious deception. With me, it is only a lascivious, tickling curiosity. Oooof course . . . *(He is caressing a flower.)* since I am slothful and self-indulgent, my tinkering often does end in something calculated to make me more comfortable in this rough world. And my friends. Damnation, where is she? *(Tosses down flower. Begins to exit to house.)*

CABANIS: Papa, didn't you say that the balloon could mean the end of wars? (FRANKLIN *is gone.)* A new age. That's what it is.

ACT ONE

Silence as they look after FRANKLIN. CABANIS *has moved as if to follow.*

TURGOT: He's leaving France. Tomorrow.

MORELLET: He's heard from his son.

CABANIS: (*Pause.*) He won't leave. (*Runs after* FRANKLIN.) Papa!

TURGOT: (*Shaking his head.*) Cabanis. (*Beat.*) How is she.

ROCHE: She seems fine. There's even a gleam about her. But she was up walking all night again. She didn't sleep.

TURGOT: Her health will break.

ROCHE: He won't leave. It's unthinkable. Our whole life will change.

MORELLET: Change, yes.

ROCHE: I weep when I walk in the garden.

MORELLET: Turgot looks forward to the departure.

TURGOT: I? Of course not. I'll feel the loss as much as anyone.

MORELLET: Turgot will have Madame to himself.

TURGOT: Hardly to myself. With the two of you forever at table.

MORELLET: True. But if they should marry?

TURGOT: (*Quick, sharp.*) He's not right for her. (*Pause.*) All I want is to get her through the evening without more pain. (*Goes out to garden.*)

MORELLET: (*Pause as* TURGOT *leaves.*) And Turgot makes three.

ROCHE: Three?

MORELLET: Roaming around in that garden. (*Counts them on his fingers.*) Papa looking for Anne. Cabanis, as usual, on Papa's coattail. And Turgot . . . putting himself between.

ROCHE: What about our pain? How are we to get through the evening?

MORELLET: Wouldn't it be funny if she wasn't even out there? (*Sees* ROCHE *drooping.*) Through the evening? We'll . . . go over old times, I suppose. (*Pause.*) Now, now

ACT ONE

... (*Puts hand on his shoulder to comfort him.*) ... think of the best that could happen. (*Beat. Carefully, as though explaining.*) Papa has heard from his son.

ROCHE: William. From England?

MORELLET: Yes.

ROCHE: Do you think William wants . . .

MORELLET: He wants a meeting, a reconciliation, I'm sure.

ROCHE: (*Rises, delighted.*) If William would come here, to France . . .

MORELLET: Yes. It could . . . answer everything. And Papa might settle with us . . . after all.

ROCHE: (*Playfully.*) Ah hah. Of course Cabanis would get jealous. He's begun to think of himself as Papa's son.

MORELLET: (*Amused.*) Yes.

ROCHE: Do you think Papa's ready to be reconciled with William?

MORELLET: Ask him. (*Beat.*) If you dare. (*Pause.*) I think he's struggling with the idea.

ROCHE: I wish . . . If he would just talk it out. Maybe we could help to . . .

TURGOT *and* CABANIS *reenter from garden.* MORELLET *counts on his fingers.* ROCHE *laughs at him.*

MORELLET: One . . . two . . .

CABANIS: Papa thinks the balloon could mean the end of wars.

CABANIS: Papa thinks the balloon could mean the end of wars.

TURGOT: Hah. There's a practical application for you. No war. King Louis' budget could be cut by three-quarters with a single stroke. *(All laugh.)* A child's dream all the same.

CABANIS: No, Turgot, no. There's bound to be a hundred practical uses . . .

ROCHE: Don't mind him, Cabanis. The old Minister of Finance will never have done.

MORELLET: *(To* TURGOT.) You're turning sour as you age, mon ami, like a pickle. Where's your spirit?

TURGOT: What remains to me I apply full force in opposition to such addlebrains as you are.

Act One

MORELLET: Oooooo. Oooo.

TURGOT: Of course! The balloon is the beginning of something we cannot dream the end of. But what are we doing with the sacred idea? Our "tinkering" is ridiculous. It is not for us to fly. We haven't the faith left to think large enough, and dare far enough. This gilded, fringed, upholstered monstrosity is a perfect mockery of France. Too weighted down by vanities to fly. Or, if it does lift, the would-be aeronauts are terrified at the first strong breeze and plunge back to earth. We had better leave flying to Papa's innocent people. They are fearless. Whoever would fly must be pure enough to meet the sky naked and plain. *(Stomps away upstage.)*

MORELLET: Iiiiiah. Wholesale condemnation. Where does this come from?

ROCHE: The financial report, I think.

MORELLET: Ah . . .

CABANIS: *(Following* TURGOT *upstage.)* Turgot, it's not true. We do have spirit. We can change.

MORELLET: *(To* ROCHE, *downstage.)* I'm not surprised. Regulating the grain trade has never worked before. They should have followed our plan.

ROCHE: I don't understand Turgot. That report looked hopeful to me.

MORELLET: You have to learn to look between lines, Roche. The figures are merely a fine fabrication. Salve for the sick at heart.

CABANIS *moves back to them.*

MORELLET: The revolutionary returns. Well? Have you convinced Turgot to throw over the court? Vive le revolution!

ROCHE: *(Interrupting to quiet* MORELLET.) Have you finished sorting Papa's papers for me to translate?

MORELLET: Yes. He's heard from his son.

ROCHE: William? From England.

MORELLET: Yes.

CABANIS: Is he coming here?

MORELLET: I don't know.

ROCHE: It would simplify my work. The biography is full of holes.

MORELLET: Ask Cabanis to fill you in, Roche. He wears Papa thin with questions. And never tires of listening. Fatal to the secrets of an old man dreaming.

CABANIS: No, no . . . Lately, when I feel closest to him, and I ask him about William . . . he turns cold without warning. Stares at me. Sometimes I almost think . . . he might strike me.

MORELLET: *(Pause. Looks at* ROCHE.*)* Could it be he finds your questions . . . impertinent.

CABANIS: No . . . How could that be. He allows me everything.

MORELLET: And what about the Loyalists quarrel?

CABANIS: I think that's forgotten. But I still don't understand it.

TURGOT: *(Moving to them.)* A quarrel?

MORELLET: Yes. Listen, Turgot. Our young Cabanis got into it with Papa about his stand on the Loyalist's property in America.

TURGOT: *(Apprehensive.)* No . . .

MORELLET: Oh, yes.

CABANIS: All I said was "What if we had a revolution here in France. And when it was over, the side that won . . . stole everything . . . that had belonged to the side that lost."

MORELLET: He went on at great length about how the gentlemanly thing would have been to give the Loyalists some reparations as part of the peace treaty.

ACT ONE

TURGOT: My god.

ROCHE: I tried to stop him.

MORELLET: Roche kept trying to change the subject.

CABANIS: Well, I still don't see it. The other American ambassadors wanted to make reparations. Papa was the only one opposed. Why should he want to . . .

TURGOT: *(To* MORELLET *and* ROCHE.) What did he say?

ROCHE: Nothing.

MORELLET: He left the room. He went home.

FRANKLIN *enters.*

FRANKLIN: I'll be damned if she's out in the garden. I've met seven cats, four sheep, two deer, a peacock, six ducks, and a rooster. And in this rain. Damnation. Hasn't been here?

MORELLET: Settle down, Papa. Come in.

FRANKLIN *is going off again.*

CABANIS: Is your son coming here, Papa?

FRANKLIN *stops dead. Pause. Singing from off:* "Last May a fine wooer."

FRANKLIN: She's here.

HELVETIUS *appears. Sees* FRANKLIN. *Pleased, comes in to greet him.* ROCHE *stands.*

HELVETIUS: Ah, Franklin, helas! Morellet was sure to bring you home in his pocket. *(She kisses him on both cheeks.)* Helas, Turgot. *(Kisses* TURGOT.) Cabanis has been catechizing his favorite mentor?

TURGOT: No. *I* am not his favorite mentor; I've lost him as well.

FRANKLIN: *(Grabbing her hand.)* Messieurs, I give you Notre Dame d'Auteuil. I would have kept her to myself, but, alas, she loves you all and would not be found.

HELVETIUS: *(Laughs and kisses his forehead.)* My wren is about to hatch and she's been so much off the nest . . . Cabanis, will you bring the drink, please. *(He exits.)* I was afraid, with the storm, that she might . . . *(Sees balloon.)* Oh, Franklin! You didn't tell me you had here a machine.

FRANKLIN: I'd tell you nothing till I had you safely in the air. And then you'd tell *me* your wrens were given wings because they have business to fly.

HELVETIUS: Aaaaah. It's the "balloon."

ROCHE: Morellet brought it. It's an exact replica.

HELVETIUS: It looks very silly, Morellet.

MORELLET: Only a report, Madame. I always trail behind.

HELVETIUS: And, Monsieur Franklin, if my wren made such messes on earth as you with your armies, she'd have no business to fly away, either.

FRANKLIN: You're not going to tell me that jungle you keep out there is innocent? It masks brutal treacheries. The ruthless jay lurking and lusting to suck the eggs of your silly wren.

MORELLET: Are we having tea, now?

HELVETIUS: Ah, but the jay is so beautiful.

TURGOT: Umhmm. Voila! Not morality, or even life, but sensual pleasure rules that garden.

HELVETIUS: As you will.

FRANKLIN: That *jungle.*

HELVETIUS: As *you* will. Still, it holds more truth than all your books and machines put together.

CABANIS *enters with tray, wine, glasses.*

ACT ONE

FRANKLIN: Vive le vin! Away with science. Let only the ancient and natural passions reign.

FRANKLIN *attaches balloon to a drop line. It rises and hangs above them.* FRANKLIN *pours for everyone.* HELVETIUS *sits downstage of table.*

ROCHE: Doctor, pardon me, but I think the passion of Icarus must be termed ancient.

FRANKLIN: True. But, my dear, dear Abbe, Icarus could not advance. Because, you see, in the society of his time, they had not such an abundance of . . . hot air.

All laugh.

MORELLET: I thought we were having tea.

FRANKLIN: *(To* HELVETIUS.*)* Your jungle still lacks a scarlet bird.

HELVETIUS: Your cardinals! Have they arrived? From Connec-ti-cut.

FRANKLIN: No. No . . . it's as before. They've all died on the crossing.

HELVETIUS: You musn't send again. If they can't survive the journey . . .

FRANKLIN: Their song is so glorious. I wanted to give you . . .

CABANIS: Roche has an announcement. Give it here.

ROCHE: Cabanis . . .

CABANIS: No. It's important. You thought he was swamped just writing your biography, but . . .

ROCHE: *(Bringing out manuscript.)* I've finished the first of the translations, that's all.

HELVETIUS: Magnificient! You must have worked through the night.

ROCHE: I was restless.

CABANIS: I'm the only one sleeping soundly here, *(Looks meaningfuly at* HELVETIUS. *Takes manuscript from* ROCHE.)

ROCHE: What with the balloon . . .

CABANIS: *(Reading.)* The Constitution of Massa . . . Massa . . .

MORELLET: Chusetts.

TURGOT *takes manuscript to look at it.*

FRANKLIN: You see, Morellet, you musn't nag him. Sitting quietly in the library, he'll outstrip us all.

ROCHE: He just thinks I should be more . . . active.

TURGOT: *(Examining manuscript.)* Not the function of a scholar. Or an historian, either, I suppose. At the right moment, this could create plenty of action.

HELVETIUS: *(To* TURGOT.) I read the first section as soon as he'd finished it. Their governing body is very like your idea for provincial assemblies.

MORELLET: I thought we were having tea, a l'Anglais . . .

ROCHE: I'll start Pennsylvania tomorrow.

MORELLET: Tea for the Doctor? For Papa?

CABANIS: Nothing to do with the Doctor. The honorable Abbe Morellet simply has missed his quota of cream.

MORELLET: And muffins with butter.

FRANKLIN: Last time I came for *breakfast* there was no butter, not to mention no lady, at home. Oooof course, if I'd stayed the night . . .

HELVETIUS: Aaaah, Franklin.

FRANKLIN: If these three can stay every night . . .

HELVETIUS: You said you'd forgiven me. I really forgot you were coming.

Act One

FRANKLIN: Me. She forgot me. Consolation.

He rises as to toast, but starts singing drinking song he has taught them.

HELVETIUS: *(Speaks as he sings, after two lines of the song.)* Besides, the good Abbe gave you all the breakfast you deserved.

FRANKLIN *addresses the first verse to* HELVETIUS. *She may answer with the chorus. Others may join him on second verse.* TURGOT, *who pours another drink, can lead third,* MORELLET *alone on fourth. Raucous and hearty.*

Fair Venus calls; her voice obey,
In beauty's arms spend night and day.
The joys of love all joys excell,
And loving's certainly doing well.

Oh No!
Not so!
For honest souls know
Friends and a bottle still bear the bell.

Then let us get money, like bees lay up honey;
We'll build us new hives and store each cell.
The sight of our treasure shall yield us great pleasure;
We'll count it, and drink it, and jingle it well.

Oh no! (etc.)

If this does not fit ye, let's govern the city;
In power is pleasure no tongue can tell;
By crowds tho you're teased, your pride shall be pleased,
And this can make Lucifer happy in hell.

Oh no! (etc.)

Then toss off your glasses, and scorn the dull asses,
Who missing the kernel still gnaw the shell;
What's love, rule or riches: Wise Solomon teaches
They're vanity, vanity vanity, still.

That's true!
He knew!

He tried them all through.
Friends and a bottle still bore the bell.

MORELLET: *(As song ends.)* By next month, perhaps, we'll have the honor to receive your son, Papa.

FRANKLIN *looks at him. All but* HELVETIUS *are startled. Pause. Then* FRANKLIN *moves to get another drink.*

MORELLET: The song made me remember. You composed it together, didn't you.

HELVETIUS: William. Is your William coming, Franklin? Oooola.

FRANKLIN: I think not.

HELVETIUS: Franklin!

FRANKLIN: It's more likely we will meet in England. On my way home.

MORELLET: *(Crossing to pour another drink.)* No more o' that, my lord. No more o' that.

HELVETIUS: You won't leave us, I know that.

FRANKLIN: *(Gets chair to sit beside her.)* I don't want to.

HELVETIUS: You must bring him here. Is he like you?

ROCHE: Impossible. There couldn't be another.

CABANIS: I know, I know! He's tall. And very handsome. God, to have grown up with you . . .

FRANKLIN: No we're not alike.

HELVETIUS: Tall and very handsome. With a gypsy mother, perhaps?

TURGOT: He worked with you, though. All the experiments . . .

FRANKLIN: *(Answering* HELVETIUS.) Perhaps.

ACT ONE

MORELLET: His mother's a secret.

CABANIS: A secret?

HELVETIUS: A gypsy. Bold and beautiful.

CABANIS: *(Stunned.)* Then he's not . . . legitimate.

ROCHE: *(Pause. Changing subject.) There* was a new age. "They tamed the lightning."

TURGOT: *(Laughing.)* Yes, but did they?

CABANIS: Is that why . . .

ROCHE: They did. And with a toy kite.

CABANIS: *(Eagerly.)* He was about as old as me then.

He is setting up a pantomime. The others understand.

TURGOT: Today, your timorous aeronauts were terrified.

CABANIS: *(To* FRANKLIN.*)* Wasn't he?

FRANKLIN: Yes . . . He was twenty, twenty-two . . .

CABANIS: I could be him. Come, Morellet. A pantomime. Play Papa for me. Come.

MORELLET: No, nonono. I'm the follower.

ROCHE: You've been elected to the Academy, Morellet.

MORELLET: Only last month. I'm still fresh at it. Turgot is our only original scientist. His experiments in steel-making far outweigh . . . *(Going back to his chair.)*

CABANIS *approaches* TURGOT *to get him to "Play"* FRANKLIN.

TURGOT: You need a storm.

CABANIS: We have one. Let's go outside.

FRANKLIN: No. No, it really is dangerous.

CABANIS: All right, then: We're sitting around restless on a rainy day . . .

HELVETIUS: *(Pause.)* Play with him yourself, Franklin.

CABANIS: Please, Papa, will you? Just . . . for tonight.

FRANKLIN *looks at* HELVETIUS, *nods, gets up.*

CABANIS: We were restless on a rainy day.

FRANKLIN: No. We'd been planning for months.

FRANKLIN *draws* CABANIS *upstage for a conference.* TURGOT *gets a chair.*

ROCHE: *(Behind* HELVETIUS.*)* Madame . . .

HELVETIUS: *(Startled.)* What.

ROCHE: Have you . . . forgotten your shawl.

HELVETIUS: Oh. *(Pause.)* Yes. Yes, I have. *(Pause.)* Oh, Roche.

ROCHE: I know, don't worry.

HELVETIUS: I feel so . . .

FRANKLIN: *(From upstage.)* Ready?

ROCHE: You look radiant.

CABANIS: Yes. We're waiting for the next storm.

FRANKLIN: And it comes.

Thunder. Lights darken. CABANIS *and* FRANKLIN *move downstge to "act out" scene. The others sit and become their audience.*

CABANIS: *(As* WILLIAM. *Eagerly.)* There it is. Shall we go now.

FRANKLIN: Yes. Get the kite. (CABANIS *moves upstage to get "kite" they will mime.)* Don't let Deborah see you. *(He stands as at door, looking at storm.)* My god, it's a beauty.

Act One

CABANIS *joins him downstage, miming kite. They step out into the storm, walking in place.*

FRANKLIN: *(Loud, over storm.)* Is the wire still fast to the top?

CABANIS: [WILLIAM] *(Mimes checking a stiff wire, about a foot long. Nods.)* Yes. Shall I put it up? *(He is ready to run with the kite.)*

FRANKLIN: *(Shouting.)* No. *(Calmer.)* Haven't you any fear. *(Mimes taking a ribbon out of his pocket.)*

CABANIS: [WILLIAM] No, Father. It's too exciting to think.

FRANKLIN: Give me the string. (CABANIS *hands the end to him; he ties the ribbon to it.)* This ribbon is silk. Hold on to it only. Don't touch the string for any reason. Do you understand?

CABANIS: [William] Yes, Father.

FRANKLIN: If I'm right . . . if I'm right, the silk should be some protection. *(Pause.)* Go ahead.

CABANIS *runs with the kite, mimes putting it into the air. He moves freely up and down stage amid chairs of his audience. They watch him.* FRANKLIN *goes to* HELVETIUS. *Takes her hand.*

HELVETIUS: You trusted him.

FRANKLIN: As no one else. *(Pause.)* With my soul. *(Shouting.)* All right, bring it here. *(He moves back into pantomime.)*

CABANIS: [WILLIAM] *(Coming back to him, out of breath.)* She's diving a lot. Wind's so stiff up there. Hard to hold her steady.

FRANKLIN: *(Getting out twine and key.)* I don't think that will matter. Give me the kite. (CABANIS *carefully hands it to him.)* And hold on to this key. (FRANKLIN *is a moment getting the feel of the kite.)* Now. Give me the key. I'll tie it to the string.

CABANIS *hands him the key.* FRANKLIN *stands holding it, not moving.*

CABANIS: [WILLIAM] *(Pause.)* Father.

FRANKLIN: *(Still not moving.)* Yes.

CABANIS: [WILLIAM] Father . . . are you all right.

FRANKLIN: *(Pause.)* You've seen me unconscious in the laboratory, Billy. You've seen animals dead from a tiny charge. *(Pause.)* What do you suppose this could do to us. If I'm right?

CABANIS: [WILLIAM] *(Not a question. He is thinking it through.)* If lightning is the same as electricity.

FRANKLIN: Yes.

CABANIS: [WILLIAM] Burned . . . charred . . . hulks. Are you frightened?

FRANKLIN: *(Shouting.)* Of course I'm frightened. If your wits weren't wet, you'd run screaming home.

CABANIS: [WILLIAM] *(Pause.)* I just think . . . that if we're supposed to die now, we will.

FRANKLIN: *(Quickly fastening the key to the twine.)* Fatalist!

FRANKLIN *takes kite string and walks into storm. Thunder, lightning. He looks to sky then touches his knuckle to the key. Shouts.*

FRANKLIN: Nothing yet.

More thunder. CABANIS *runs to him, looking at the string.*

CABANIS: [WILLIAM] Look. The twine. The threads are standing out. Look.

FRANKLIN *looks at it. Slowly puts knuckle to key. Feels shock. Shouts.*

FRANKLIN: That's it. That's it. *(Takes knuckle away, puts it back, feels shock again.)* My god. We're right. That's it.

CABANIS: [WILLIAM] *(Puts knuckle on key. Shouts.)* Aaaaahh. *(Laughing.)* Aaaaahh.

Both laugh, hug each other. Thunder grows to peak and stops. Others

ACT ONE

stand, shout "Brava" and applaud. They surround the performers and chatter all at once.

CABANIS: *(As himself.)* Is that it? Did I find him? God, what life. What life.

HELVETIUS: Is that your Billy, Franklin. How did he do.

FRANKLIN: *(Drawing her aside.)* How did I do. Are you my Anne-Catherine?

HELVETIUS: Franklin, you musn't . . .

TURGOT: *(To* CABANIS.) In those days, my dear young physician, you weren't even anybody's dream of bliss.

CABANIS: No?

FRANKLIN: *(To* HELVETIUS.) Musn't what.

HELVETIUS: Please.

TURGOT: Perhaps you were a squall. Or a soiled diaper. If anything.

CABANIS: Let's do another, Papa. Come on.

ROCHE: That was before the Seven Years' War.

HELVETIUS: *(Rejoining group.)* A Frenchman had actually proven electricity a month earlier.

TURGOT: Even we had a chance left . . . for spirit then.

ROCHE: But he was using Papa's instructions.

FRANKLIN: *(To* ROCHE.) You mean the French and Indian War. We foxed you there.

MORELLET: Don't puff yourself up, venerable sage. You were a minor front.

CABANIS: Come on, Papa. Another . . . from when you went to England.

FRANKLIN: *(Drawing her by the hand.)* Come, Madame.

HELVETIUS: *(Resisting.)* Franklin . . .

FRANKLIN: Just for a breath . . . of the storm. I'm going to miss your wren.

FRANKLIN *and* HELVETIUS *exit. The others watch them and look at each other. Only* CABANIS' *line of thought is not interrupted.*

CABANIS: A bastard. My god. William Franklin is a bastard. *(Looks at others.)* And? He treated him as his heir, didn't he? Took him to London to study law?

ROCHE: Yes. When he was appointed agent of the Pennsylvania Assembly to Parliament.

CABANIS: Morellet, you knew them then.

MORELLET: Yes.

CABANIS: If William would come here now . . .

MORELLET: Yes. *(Looking at* TURGOT.*)* Many things might . . . be settled.

ROCHE: But would Papa see him?

MORELLET: That's true.

CABANIS: See him. Why not? *(Pause. Looking at others.)* Why shouldn't he see him.

MORELLET: Well . . . *(He looks at* ROCHE. ROCHE *nods "yes".)* Roche keeps more orderly accounts than I. I just keep remembering the Lippencot affair.

CABANIS: Lippencot. What are you talking about.

ROCHE: It was . . . I suppose you would call it an . . . international incident. It's a long story and very complicated, but . . .

CABANIS: Mon dieu. What does it have to do with Dr. Franklin?

MORELLET: No, nonono. It was William it had to do with. It's just that the embarrassment . . .

CABANIS: For god's sake, tell it, will you, Roche.

Act One

ROCHE: Well. Towards the end of the American war feelings got extremely bitter between Americans—rebels and loyalists. One night a raiding party of Loyalists led by a Captain Lippencot strung up a rebel soldier. They left him hanging with a note pinned to his body, their ensignia on it. Very nasty. And quite illegal, not to say immoral. Local rebels were enraged. For a while it threatened to erupt into a wanton exchange of murders. Washington needed a bold action to curb the ... passions, so ... he held a lottery. Among the British prisoners of war. One of them would be executed in place of Lippencot. The "winner" was nineteen years old. A pretty nobleman, Captain Asgill.

CABANIS: Who had no crime but defending his king.

MORELLET: Exactly.

CABANIS: Very ugly.

MORELLET: Very.

CABANIS: Did they do it?

MORELLET: That wasn't the idea. Washington informed the British that they were *going* to do it.

ROCHE: The object was to get Lippencot turned over for trial, to bring the whole savage affair under the jurisdiction of law.

CABANIS: Wait. Asgill ... Asgill ...

ROCHE: They set a time.

MORELLET: Captain Asgill, it turned out, had very loving parents.

ROCHE: They went to their influential friends. They went to King George. They wrote to General Washington.

MORELLET: But the same answer came back. Turn over Lippencot.

ROCHE: They got very desperate. King George even appealed to King Louis.

CABANIS: That's it. Two enemy monarchs pleading for the same boy. I remember. A hostage. Ransom.

ROCHE: One man's life paid for another isn't ransom.

MORELLET: Very high-running blood.

ROCHE: The stand regarding Lippencot was that he was only a soldier, too, following orders.

MORELLET: Louis put pressure on Papa, as well, but Papa held the line: Turn over the responsible party.

CABANIS: But if Lippencot *was* following orders, then who was responsi . . .

ROCHE: Exactly.

MORELLET: The affair had gotten out of hand. Washington was totally sick of it. But he had proved his strength. Or at least his leverage.

ROCHE: Revenge carried to such an extreme became ridiculous. The whole warring world, it seemed, was crying out for mercy, for forgiveness . . .

CABANIS: The issue wasn't revenge, though, it was justice.

MORELLET: You can separate them?

CABANIS: *(Pause.)* Then they couldn't determine the responsible party.

MORELLET: Oh, they could have, but, by then . . . It was very messy . . .

CABANIS: Well, who had given Lippencot his orders?

TURGOT: *(Pause.)* William. William Franklin.

CABANIS *stunned. Silence.* FRANKLIN *and* HELVETIUS *enter upstage with umbrella.*

FRANKLIN: No chance of a moon.

Act One   23

CABANIS: *(Sotto vocce.)* God. Did Papa know?

MORELLET *and* ROCHE *shrug or do not answer.*

FRANKLIN: It's set to storm the whole damned night.

TURGOT: *(Moving to take* HELVETIUS' *arm.)* But your lightning rod will keep us snug, yes, Papa?

CABANIS: *(Trying to set up another pantomime.)* London, now, Papa. Let's do London. I'm William. I've stayed late at a lecture at the Inns of Court.

FRANKLIN: *(Laughing at him.)* Have you.

CABANIS: Yes, and you've been waiting. You've got important news for me.

FRANKLIN: Oho. You know about that, do you?

CABANIS: Of course I do. You're getting old, Papa. You forget which stories you've told me.

FRANKLIN: *(Looking at him sharply.)* And which . . . I haven't.

HELVETIUS: In London you nested with the Stevensons.

MORELLET: Ah yes. Margaret Stevenson. Your wife away from wife. *(Pause. Others are embarrassed.)* You play her, Anne.

FRANKLIN: Not at all. Never do. Not at all. Mistress Margaret Stevenson was a plump house-frau like my own dear Deborah. Not to be played *(taking her hand)* by a queen. *(They move downstage together.)*

TURGOT: *(Encouraging the pantomime.)* Go ahead, Cabanis.

CABANIS: *(As* WILLIAM.*)* Sorry I'm late, Father. I think the professor went to sleep talking.

HELVETIUS: *(Still with* FRANKLIN.*)* Maybe I could be her svelte daughter Polly. Which did you love best? *(She arranges two chairs for them downstage.)*

CABANIS: [WILLIAM] Sorry, Father . . .

FRANKLIN: *(To* HELVETIUS.*)* As always, my flower: I gave each all she would take.

CABANIS: [WILLIAM] The professor went to sleep talking.

FRANKLIN: *(Finally answering* CABANIS.*)* I daresay he made more sense asleep than awake.

HELVETIUS: *(To* CABANIS.*)* No, go away. You aren't home yet. I'll be Polly.

FRANKLIN: *(Suddenly holds her. She responds. He shouts.)* Billy!

CABANIS: *(Perplexed, he turns to the others.)* What?

TURGOT: Might as well let her play Polly. *(Goes upstage to sit.)*

FRANKLIN: Billy! William!

CABANIS *shrugs and steps upstage out of the "playing" area.* FRANKLIN *paces.*

ROCHE: *(To* MORELLET.*)* What news does he have?

HELVETIUS: *(As* POLLY.*)* Sit down, Papa. *(She sits in chair she has prepared, love-seat fashion.)*

MORELLET: I'm not sure.

HELVETIUS: [POLLY] He's not here yet.

FRANKLIN: Not here. How could he not be here? *(Looks at* CABANIS.*)*

HELVETIUS: [POLLY] Sit with me. I'll tell you a secret.

FRANKLIN: *(Coming to her.)* Shame on you. Wily woman. All right, tell me.

HELVETIUS: [POLLY] Sit first.

FRANKLIN: Shameless! *(He sits.).*

HELVETIUS: [POLLY] You won't tell? Not even my mother.

FRANKLIN: Especially not. *Why* not.

ACT ONE

HELVETIUS: [POLLY] Because she'd be much too excited if she knew.

FRANKLIN: If she knew . . . what, minx.

HELVETIUS: [POLLY] If she knew that someone very, very dear is thinking of settling here.

FRANKLIN: *(Mocking.)* No.

TURGOT: *(From upstage, surprised.)* No.

CABANIS: *(From upstage.)* Did he want . . . ?

MORELLET: *(From upstage.)* Oh, yes. He wanted to . . .

HELVETIUS: [POLLY] *(To FRANKLIN.)* Yes! Here in Britain—for good. His son Billy told me so it must be true. *(As herself.)* Wasn't it, wasn't it true.

FRANKLIN: Clever minx . . .

HELVETIUS: [POLLY] He said your trip to Scotland settled it. That now you were determined.

FRANKLIN: Did you flirt that secret out of him?

HELVETIUS: [POLLY] . . . and then he tried to sell me three shares of "Indiana Company."

FRANKLIN: *(Gets up, laughing loudly.)* By god! He can think of nothing else. I tell you, Polly, we tromped about those gorgeous, succulent highlands, and all he could say was "Father, the west of America is like this; the frontier called Indiana is even more beautiful." He wants that land so much . . . *(he stops, suddenly lost)* so much . . . *(Uncertain who he is speaking to.)* Polly. Polly, you do like him.

HELVETIUS: [POLLY] *(Quietly.)* Yes, Papa.

FRANKLIN: He's had a fight from the cradle, Polly, because men could call him bastard.

CABANIS *comes toward them, listening, moved.*

FRANKLIN: Even my wife. Deborah was a saint. She took him in. But even she, yes, especially she, has a corner of her mind that hates him for living. And when that corner turns out . . . that's a vicious, painful sight.

HELVETIUS: *(Pause. As herself.)* You've loved him. He has you.

FRANKLIN: *(Sees* CABANIS. *Angrily.)* Billy! Where have you been.

CABANIS: [WILLIAM] *(Picking up his cue.)* Sorry, Father. Evening, Polly.

FRANKLIN: Isn't it wonderful!

CABANIS: [WILLIAM] Isn't what wonderful?

FRANKLIN: My news.

CABANIS: *(Impatient, as himself.)* Papa.

FRANKLIN: What?

HELVETIUS: *(As herself.)* You haven't told him yet, Franklin.

FRANKLIN: I thought he knew the story. *(Back in play.)* Take this glass in hand, Billy. *(Goes to table. Pours three drinks, hands them round as he speaks.* HELVETIUS *joins them.)* This will be the most potent drink you've ever taken.

CABANIS: [WILLIAM] *(Uncertainly.)* What is it. Some new Madiera . . . ?

FRANKLIN: I want you to cast down into your soul, Billy, and come out with a toast . . . to a young sovereign. The most virtuous, wise, discerning, and benevolent that ever man has had the fortune to serve. Give us the health and long life of his brilliant and gracious majesty—God protect him and make us ever thankful—King George III.

MORELLET: *(Moves downstage into scene.)* How time does fly.

CABANIS: [WILLIAM] *(Not understanding, but awed.)* To young King George.

Spectators convulsed with stifled laughter.

ACT ONE 27

ROCHE: *(Moves in.)* Did they really feel so?

TURGOT: *(Moves in.)* Quiet, plebian. Of course they did.

HELVETIUS: [POLLY] *(Toasting.)* King George.

Players drink. Others are now standing on the edge of the "scene".

TURGOT: We've no monopoly on sovereign worship. That love is the prop of nations. Look around. Keeps starving people proud.

Stop. Everyone waiting for FRANKLIN. *He looks at them, glass in hand.*

FRANKLIN: Well?

ROCHE: Well? What is it?

FRANKLIN: Congratulations, Billy!

All begin to respond, then stop. They still don't have the piece of information.

FRANKLIN: Long may we bend the Royal ear.

CABANIS: [WILLIAM] *(Deciding to go ahead. Excited.)* You mean . . . Have they . . . ? Do I have . . .

FRANKLIN: *(Laughing.)* You've got it, Billy. It's all yours. More than we'd dreamed. New Jersey is yours! Polly, you may shake the Governor's hand.

HELVETIUS: [POLLY] The Governorship? He got the appointment!

CABANIS: [WILLIAM] *(Stunned.)* My god. My god . . .

HELVETIUS: [POLLY] *(Shakes his hand.)* William, William, it's . . . wonderful.

FRANKLIN: Allow me to be the second . . . Governor Franklin.

CABANIS: [WILLIAM] *(They embrace.)* Father.

The others, who have surrounded them, take over.

MORELLET: Of course, of course. Governor by royal appointment. It was the first time for a colonial.

FRANKLIN: That's right.

CABANIS: [WILLIAM] *(Stays in "character", moves away from group.)* I don't believe it. I just can't believe it...

ROCHE: Hard to imagine, isn't it. Governors.

HELVETIUS: It's like your plan, Turgot.

TURGOT: It's *exactly* what we need. If we could have appointed Governors presiding over provincial assemblies...

MORELLET: Turgot, you know it's impossible. The court won't give up an inch of power.

CABANIS: [WILLIAM] *(From his position apart, draws* FRANKLIN *back into play.)* The power, Father. My god, think of the power. And between us. With you in the Pennsylvania Assembly and me in New Jersey.

FRANKLIN: Yes. *(Moves to* CABANIS. *Joins "play" again. Others notice.)*

CABANIS: [WILLIAM] This will do it, won't it. It'll get us the charter... We'll be able to get the Indiana Company approved.

FRANKLIN: As soon as your appointment is sealed, we'll push it through. Indiana, Illinois... whatever you want to call it—your west is yours, Billy.

CABANIS: [WILLIAM] It's because of you, Father. They want to claim you completely.

MORELLET: *(To* CABANIS *from sidelines; kibbutzing.)* Influence is not to sniff at. No one was ever placed without it.

FRANKLIN: Don't be silly. They know you're equal to it.

MORELLET: *(Kibbutzing.)* But to place a colonial. And, a bastard...

Act One

FRANKLIN: Well . . . yes. We must be careful . . . quiet. We don't want to give anyone a reason to . . . object . . . before you're safely in place.

CABANIS: *(Finally breaking out of scene.)* Ahaaa. How did I do? How did I do?

The others, laughing, shake his hand. FRANKLIN *is with* HELVETIUS.

MORELLET: Aha. Influence is an equivocator. It sets em on and it puts em off.

ROCHE: Voila, Turgot. Like old Maurepas talking you in and out with Louis.

MORELLET: Son of Franklin gets appointment. Franklin's son can't keep appointment.

TURGOT: No, no, nothing like.

MORELLET: But of course. In with Louis because you're honest and tough. Out, for the same reason.

TURGOT *moves away displeased.*

FRANKLIN: How about marriage? *(He picks up the scene again as a excuse to talk vicariously to* HELVETIUS.*)* While we're setting up in life . . . how about a Governor's lady.

HELVETIUS: *(Startled for an instant, then answers as* POLLY.*)* Papa!

CABANIS: [WILLIAM] *(Jumping back into scene.)* He sees my soul to the bottom, Polly. I was only waiting for respectable employment.

Focus of all shifts back to scene.

FRANKLIN: Splendid, splendid. I'll speak to Mistress Margaret in the morning. Unless you'd rather . . .

CABANIS: [WILLIAM] Father. *(Pause.)* It's not Polly I'm going to marry.

All at attention. HELVETIUS *looks at* FRANKLIN, *steps away.*

FRANKLIN: Not . . . Polly.

CABANIS: [WILLIAM] I speak, but you won't listen. My . . . interest lies elsewhere.

FRANKLIN: *(Sharply.)* We know your body lies in curious places.

CABANIS: [WILLIAM] Father!

FRANKLIN: How many bastards have you got hidden away.

TURGOT: *(From aside.)* My god, had he . . .

MORELLET: *(From aside.)* Like father, like son.

CABANIS: [WILLIAM] How many have you.

FRANKLIN: Sorry. Sorry, Billy. It's . . . bitter. *(Pause.)* Who.

CABANIS: [WILLIAM] You know who, Father. Elizabeth Downes.

FRANKLIN: Gracious, sweet-tempered girl.

CABANIS: [WILLIAM] Yes.

FRANKLIN: And well-titled.

CABANIS: [WILLIAM] Yes.

FRANKLIN: But, oh, Billy, Polly's at least as lovely. And her spirit, Billy . . . it climbs, it soars . . . and her vivacious mind . . .

CABANIS: [WILLIAM] *(Impatiently.)* Yes, yes, Father. But Polly's your love, not mine. Don't expect me to desire what you'd like to have.

FRANKLIN *is still, looking at him.*

HELVETIUS: [POLLY] *(Moving to him.)* But *you'll* stay here, Papa. You'll settle here in England.

FRANKLIN: *(Breaks out of stare and speaks passionately.)* Nothing can prevent it. If I can persuade Deborah to make the crossing. Here, in this gentle, this gracious, this glorious . . . England.

Hoots and boos from spectators. Uproar, scene is finally broken up, FRANKLIN *takes* HELVETIUS' *hand, leads her back to down right chairs.*

TURGOT: English sentiment. Grease and slop.

HELVETIUS: *(As herself.)* You were going to settle in England, Franklin. You would have transplanted yourself . . . then.

ROCHE: Did he make a good governor?

FRANKLIN: Yes . . . He did well. *(to* HELVETIUS.) It's up to you . . . where I settle now.

CABANIS: God, the power . . . creative combination. With him as governor, and you representing so many colonies in England.

FRANKLIN: Very . . . satisfying, yes. The double bond.

TURGOT: The promise of power was immense. Papa could lobby for western land while son sharpened the tools. Efficient, too.

MORELLET: But when the politics got rougher . . .

FRANKLIN: When I had to stand for colonies that were behaving defiantly . . . it was a strain.

ROCHE: Massachusetts.

FRANKLIN: Yes. Massachusetts, too.

HELVETIUS: You embarrassed William?

FRANKLIN: No doubt.

TURGOT: Embarrassed him. Crap. Why so polite. Enough slop English sentiment. I've seen their 'politicians' in action: you know the worst of our courtiers, Anne, God knows, you and I do, and it's nothing, nothing . . . *(Proclaims as he begins another pantomime.)* The Lord's Committee of his Majesty's Privy Council.

FRANKLIN *looks startled,* TURGOT *moves to side of table.*

MORELLET: Hear, hear. What's this.

TURGOT: And here's a sweet witty Scot. I give you Prosecutor Wedderburn. *(He bows, assuming character of* WEDDERBURN.*)*

MORELLET: Who's Wedderburn.

ROCHE: Lawyer. You could do him easily. Nothing but specious reasoning.

TURGOT: *(As* WEDDERBURN.*)* We will hear the petition of the Massachusetts Assembly for the removal of Governor Hutchinson. *(As himself.)* Well? Roche? Assemble the Lords. Whitehall Palace . . . in the Cockpit.

ROCHE *marshals* MORELLET *and* CABANIS *to stand with him as lords behind the table.*

TURGOT: You pitied *my* disgrace. Watch Papa.

FRANKLIN: *(Rises reluctant, but stands to "play" down right facing them.)* I come as agent of the Assembly of Massachusetts. They have instructed me to lay before you their resolution and the letters upon which . . .

TURGOT: [WEDDERBURN] Letters.

FRANKLIN: Letters upon which . . .

TURGOT: [WEDDERBURN] What letters.

FRANKLIN: . . . the resolution is based.

TURGOT: [WEDDERBURN] Letters . . . addressed to you?

FRANKLIN: *(Pause.)* No. They humbly beg . . .

TURGOT: [WEDDERBURN] To whom, then.

FRANKLIN: . . . beg that Governor Hutchinson be removed.

TURGOT: [WEDDERBURN] To the Massachusetts Assembly? *(Pause.)* No?

ACT ONE

FRANKLIN: No.

TURGOT: [WEDDERBURN] No. *(Pause.)* Then how . . . how . . . did these "letters" find their way into your hands, Doctor Franklin?

FRANKLIN *doesn't answer.*

TURGOT: [WEDDERBURN] Surely you can tell us that.

FRANKLIN: *(Pause.)* The Lords are aware . . .

TURGOT: [WEDDERBURN] Perhaps you *didn't* steal them.

FRANKLIN: That in such cases . . .

TURGOT: [WEDDERBURN] Perhaps you only stole them from the person that stole them.

Laughter. TURGOT *signals* ROCHE. LORDS *boo.*

ROCHE: *(As lord.)* Vindictive, subtle traitor.

TURGOT: [WEDDERBURN] But why should Dr. Franklin be drawn to such a disgraceful deed. Because, my Lords, poor Richard is ambitious. His little ego has been swollen by all the attention paid his coming and goings. He becomes drunk with absurd notions of grandeur, and begins to fancy himself the minister of a "great American republic", a mighty and independent power for whom he alone is qualified to speak. And that same proud minister will steal, betray, set a whole province aflame with rebellion, and all because, my Lords, he would himself be . . . Governor of Massachusetts.

HELVETIUS *stands.* LORDS *become vicious crowd. Divide lines, and/or speak in chorus.*

LORDS: *(Shouts.)* Traitor. Thief. Incendiary.

TURGOT: [WEDDERBURN] *(Building.)* I hope, my Lords, that you will mask and brand the man . . .

FRANKLIN *sits down right.*

LORDS: *(Shouts.)* Old snake. Judas. Throw him out.

TURGOT: [WEDDERBURN] *(Building.)* . . . For the glory of this country . . .

LORDS: *(Shouts.)* Throw him out. Sneak. Throw him out.

TURGOT *staggers, then turns toward* LORDS, *confused, speaks weakly.*

TURGOT: *(As himself.)* No . . . no . . . leave me alone.

LORDS: *(In their stride, haven't noticed the change in tone.)* Traitor. Thief. Incendiary.

TURGOT: *(Passionate, more definite.)* No. All I've done is for France . . . for the good of France.

LORDS: *(Shouts die, confused.)* Throw him out. Throw him . . .

TURGOT: *(Grows frenzied.)* You're bleeding France. Bleeding her. With your extravagance, your excess. You're all worth nothing, you do nothing, you produce nothing, you offer France nothing at all. You only take. I . . .

HELVETIUS *has moved to him. She touches him.*

HELVETIUS: Turgot.

TURGOT: *(Looks at her. Still blurred.)* It's all right. I outlived it. I outlived . . . disgrace. So did your husband. Disgrace . . . with us is an official category of being, it . . . wounds without maiming. But these "lords" *(Gesturing toward the others.)* these British "parliamentarians" have to fester up a fresh class of barbarism when they intend to disgrace. Voila.

TURGOT *gestures toward* FRANKLIN, *who sits, head down.* HELVETIUS *nods to* CABANIS, *goes to arrange chess set at table. He watches her, then moves to* FRANKLIN. *They will try to help him gently out of mood.* ROCHE *sits up left.*

ACT ONE

MORELLET: Good god. What barbarism.

TURGOT: Yes.

MORELLET: But Turgot, your own dismissal was not at all . . .

TURGOT: How do you know. Where were you then, mon ami? *(Pause.)* It had the same effect, but the blade wasn't rusty. Or nicked. Didn't tear.

CABANIS *begins speaking to* FRANKLIN. *He is beginning a new scene. Others note, clear upstage.* HELVETIUS *sits at table.*

MORELLET: This public baiting is . . . grotesque.

ROCHE: How could any civilized people . . . *(Breaks off to listen.)*

CABANIS: *(As* MESSENGER.*)* Dr. Franklin, Dr. Franklin. I am acquainted with a well-born lady . . . who has heard of your skill, and would like to test her own against you. At chess. If . . . it would please you . . .

FRANKLIN *drags himself to his feet.*

FRANKLIN: Thank you. I'll meet the lady.

CABANIS: [MESSENGER] *(Approaching* HELVETIUS *with* FRANKLIN.*)* Miss Howe, may I present Dr. Franklin.

HELVETIUS: *(As* MISS HOWE.*)* You honor me, Dr. Franklin. Sit down.

FRANKLIN: *(He sits.)* The honor, and the pleasure, is surely mine.

HELVETIUS: [MISS HOWE] Black or white.

FRANKLIN: White, today, I think. If you don't mind.

HELVETIUS: [MISS HOWE] *(Turning the board.)* I play on either side.

They make several moves in silence.

FRANKLIN: You play boldly. *(He moves.)*

HELVETIUS: [MISS HOWE] Only with men. I find it startles them into confusion. *(She moves and takes a piece.)* Your knight.

FRANKLIN: And does their confusion—*(he moves and takes a piece)* your bishop—loose them the game.

HELVETIUS: [MISS HOWE] *(Laughing.)* Oh no. Subtlety, like yours, is never lost.

They play in silence.

HELVETIUS: [MISS HOWE] *(Casually.)* Whatever are we to do with Britain and the colonies. I hope not civil war.

FRANKLIN: They should kiss and be friends. Quarreling is no use, and could ruin both.

HELVETIUS: [MISS HOWE] It seems to me that you should be employed in settling things. No one better.

FRANKLIN: I thank you, Madam. But . . . the ministers would never employ me in that good work. They choose rather to abuse me.

HELVETIUS: [MISS HOWE] Aye, they behaved shamefully, and some now admit to shame.

MORELLET: [As HOWE] *(Stands and speaks suddenly.)* Shamefully. Treated you shamefully. And don't think they don't realize their profound mistake. They have cut themselves off from their best, most erudite, most cultivated and worldly link with their . . . colonies.

HELVETIUS *and* FRANKLIN *are unsure what he's doing.*

MORELLET: [As HOWE] *(Giving* HELVETIUS *a cue.)* Please to introduce me . . . sister.

FRANKLIN: Aaaah. It's your brother. Admiral Howe.

MORELLET: [HOWE] *(Moving in.)* I am honored, pleased as a schoolboy to be meeting so great a man—eminent in whatever field he turns to.

Act One

FRANKLIN: Why thank you, I . . .

MORELLET: [HOWE] No, no, stay where you are. Go on with the game. I'll just . . . watch . . . the master at work.

FRANKLIN: As you wish. *(He returns to game.)*

They play. MORELLET *watches, then may pace a bit.*

MORELLET: [HOWE] How . . . to repair the terrible breach. *(Pause.)* I . . . suspect . . . that you might not wish to deal directly with the Lords after the shameful injuries they have done you . . .

FRANKLIN: *(Focusing on board.)* My injuries are nothing next to those of my country.

MORELLET: [HOWE] Quite so quite so. *(Pause.)* Perhaps . . . I might serve as a channel, indirect and secret. Perfectly secret.

TURGOT: *(From aside.)* Perfect casting.

FRANKLIN: They could just apolgize.

MORELLET: [HOWE] Ahh, yes. But you see . . . So many distinguished men . . . having displayed their . . . passions so forcefully . . .

FRANKLIN: *(Breaking in.)* Quite so quite so.

MORELLET: Yes, yes. *(Pause.)* What do you think of . . . someone . . . going to America to inquire into their grievances . . . on the spot.

FRANKLIN: *(Still not looking up.)* The right person could be of great use.

HELVETIUS: [MISS HOWE] *(Impulsively, to* MORELLET.) I wish you were going. I'd like that much better than our brother commanding an army there.

Play stops. Pause.

FRANKLIN: I think, Madam, some more honorable employment should be found for . . . General Howe.

MORELLET: [HOWE] *(Hastily.)* Be assured, Dr. Franklin, the only desire of both my brother and me is a peaceful solution to the present . . . unrest. And we are prepared to expend all our energies to bring about such a solution. We firmly believe that the colonies are to be treated as beloved, though wayward, children, rather than as . . . the enemy.

FRANKLIN *sits silent.*

MORELLET: [HOWE] Among men of the world, what are a few . . . letters misplaced . . . Certainly no cause for alarm . . .

FRANKLIN: *(Looks at him.)* You accept that I stole . . .

MORELLET: [HOWE] *(Breaking in)* Tell me, *(Bringing out manuscript. Same as* ROCHE'S *translation. It is being used as prop)* do you know this?

FRANKLIN: You have my paper?

MORELLET: [HOWE] *(Reads.)* "Hints for producing a more Durable Union between Britain and the Colonies."

FRANKLIN: Then you know already what I think should be done.

MORELLET: Ah, yes . . .

FRANKLIN *returns to playing chess.*

MORELLET: [HOWE] It is, perhaps, a bit . . . naive. *(Pause)* Perhaps you might . . . reconsider . . . and formulate another plan. One more . . . acceptable . . . to the Lords. *(Pause.)* The magnitude of the service you would be doing the nation is incalculable. *(Pause.)* Of course, I would never attempt to influence you by any appeal to selfish motives. Nevertheless . . . you could expect, for such a service, any reward in the power of the government to bestow.

FRANKLIN *rises suddenly, upsetting some of the chess pieces in his agitation. He takes the paper and leaves.*

ACT ONE

FRANKLIN: I'm sorry. I'm sorry. Excuse me, please.

TURGOT: *(Standing.)* Now, who dares call Louis treacherous.

MORELLET: I fear Louis hasn't the wit for treachery.

FRANKLIN *staggers downstage. All are alarmed, stand and move toward him, uncertain how to proceed.*

FRANKLIN: *(A cry, may not even raise his head.)* Son.

CABANIS *looks at others, hesitates.* HELVETIUS *may touch him, nod. He moves to* FRANKLIN. *Others move away to allow them space, but remain alert and standing.*

FRANKLIN: Son.

CABANIS: [As WILLIAM] Father. *(They embrace.)*

FRANKLIN: Exquisite home, you have, William.

CABANIS: [WILLIAM] You've been too long away.

FRANKLIN: New Jersey could never mistake you for a printer's son.

CABANIS: [WILLIAM] They tried to burn your house.

FRANKLIN: *(Pause.)* The Stamp Act.

CABANIS: [WILLIAM] Yes. It's a nightmare here.

FRANKLIN: Yes.

CABANIS: [WILLIAM] What will you do.

FRANKLIN: *(Pause.)* Elizabeth looks well.

ROCHE: *(From aside.)* So he did take Elizabeth.

FRANKLIN: The people adore her.

CABANIS: [WILLIAM] Yes.

FRANKLIN: The Governor's lady.

Silence.

FRANKLIN: What do you think of the new name for our western charter.

CABANIS: [WILLIAM] Are you mocking me? The Indiana Company, the Illinois, the Grand Ohio, the farther half of the moon, I loose track.

FRANKLIN: Walpole Associates. The amount of blue blood that's signed on since . . .

CABANIS: [WILLIAM] *(Sharply.)* Do you think you're fooling someone?

FRANKLIN: No. Only outweighing them. Since Walpole lent his name, the list is starting to read like a Knights of the Garter roll.

CABANIS: [WILLIAM] How can the list be approved with the name "Franklin" on it?

FRANKLIN: *(Pause.)* I got out, William. As soon as the Governor Hutchinson mess was apparent. I resigned my stock to clear the company of my name.

CABANIS: [WILLIAM] While the Iroquois spend my money.

FRANKLIN: You already bought . . . ?

CABANIS: [WILLIAM] 50,000 acres. Around Lake Otsego. *(Pause.)* You wrote that ratification was certain.

CABANIS *walks away. Silence.*

CABANIS: [WILLIAM] Will you marry Margaret Stevenson now?

FRANKLIN: Deborah . . .

CABANIS: [WILLIAM] She knew she'd never see you again.

FRANKLIN: You wrote that the snow . . .

CABANIS: [WILLIAM] Severe wind. I arrived barely in time for interment. *(Pause.)* Will you marry Margaret Stevenson now?

FRANKLIN: At my age?

Act One

CABANIS: [WILLIAM] That hasn't deterred you from playing the husband. I'm sure she expects it.

FRANKLIN: Well, Billy, I . . .

CABANIS: [WILLIAM] *(Laughing.)* You see, I still know you. Come, let's drink. *(Moves to table, pours. They sit.)* To your safe return.

FRANKLIN: Safe. Tell you a secret. This old man, in one weak moment, wished never to come safe ashore. It's soothing . . . the isolation, out there . . . a sea cradle, out of time, endless calm.

CABANIS: [WILLLIAM] It's time to rest, Father.

FRANKLIN: It should be. It should be. *(Pause.)* I spent most of the month afloat writing. *(Brings out manuscript.)* Started "Dear Son" and had a bit of trouble cutting off. Describes the last "secret" negotiations.

CABANIS *begins to page through it. Others relax. Some may sit.*

CABANIS: [WILLIAM] Nothing is secret here for long. Best friends are traitors by nightfall. *(Pause.)* What do you want to say.

FRANKLIN: Your council of governors idea didn't . . . ?

CABANIS: [WILLIAM] There was no chance. Most of them have been less able to keep control, even than I. The 'governors' just . . . ran away.

FRANKLIN: Billy . . . I know there's been madness on this side, too, but . . .

CABANIS: [WILLIAM] There is no freedom of choice here. Only of rebellion. I try to find a quiet path for bewildered people.

FRANKLIN: Bewildered, yes. *(Pause.)* The last day I was in London, I sat going over a stack of colony newspapers, with Joseph Priestly, picking out articles that might do us some good if they were reprinted in England. And . . . I embarrassed myself. Often I . . . couldn't go on, for the tears that kept running down my face . . . freely . . . as if . . . there would be no end to them. *(Pause.)* So much bewilderment, so much frustration, for so long. Chatham in front of the House of Lords with his plan of reconciliation. If you'd seen the contempt they hurled at him, that brilliant man.

CABANIS: [WILLIAM] Brilliant men are not always to the point. *(Pause.)* My responsibility is direct. It is responsibility for these people, and to them, and to the King. They know where I am and they know that they can depend on me to be there. Where are you?

FRANKLIN: *(Pause.)* They say there's an army gathering at Boston.

CABANIS: [WILLIAM] You remember all the "army" we could rustle to defend the frontier.

FRANKLIN: They held together once we pointed out their noses.

CABANIS: [WILLIAM] Against Indians.

FRANKLIN: *(Pointed.)* Washington's handing out officer's commissions. *(Pause.)* I was a Colonel that day, remember? That scrawny muddy fort.

CABANIS: [WILLIAM] Stirling accepted a commission. I threw him off my council.

FRANKLIN: You were a dashing Captain. Barely nineteen. *(Pause.)* They made Stirling a Brigadier General. *(Pause. Attempting to stir him.)* There's a favorite joke around London about us. They say it would take only a thousand grenadiers to go from one end of America to the other and geld all the males. Partly by force and partly . . . by a little coaxing.

CABANIS: [WILLIAM] *(Pause, quietly.)* Where are you, Father.

FRANKLIN: Billy . . . I've struggled a long bitter time over this.

CABANIS: [WILLIAM] You flit here and there, are never to be pinned down, accept responsibility only to yourself, yet declare

ACT ONE 43

yourself at the people's service.

FRANKLIN: You know that I am.

CABANIS: [WILLIAM] *(Standing.)* You make yourself a little god. A potentate not answerable to anyone. You operate always outside the laws set down for other men. And because you are clever, yes, and strong, and because the world is wide and offers you continuously fresh parties upon whom to play, you, one way and another, prosper. Yes. You have done the people—mankind even—much service. But your omniscient view of yourself, your pride, your ego, make you more dangerous to men's real freedom than the most obvious tyrant. Because you pretend humility, while his colors are known.

FRANKLIN: Not pretend. Use. I would have said I "use" humility.

CABANIS: [WILLIAM] Yes, use. Use. But it is the one thing that you have no true ounce of.

FRANKLIN: Billy, you know how I have loved England.

CABANIS: [WILLLIAM] Pity the man who crosses you.

FRANKLIN: William.

CABANIS: [WILLIAM] It's true.

FRANKLIN: You know I have loved her, but she has betrayed us on every . . .

CABANIS: [WILLIAM] *(Moves, agitated.)* Don't tell me England has betrayed the colonies. England's mistake was in humiliating you. Your mother country slapped you down, and now you can't rest, you'll never rest, until she has felt your revenge. You rise enraged and want to change the world. And all, you will say, in the service of the people. But which people? Which country. Is it for the good of the American colonies to offer civil war to England. Look at us. No army, navy, weapons, officers, industry, government, nothing.

MORELLET: *(From aside.)* It's true.

CABANIS: [WILLIAM] If this war comes we will be wiped away.

Silence.

FRANKLIN: You begin to feel it in your legs.

CABANIS: [WILLIAM] My legs.

FRANKLIN: I've noticed it in a few . . . others. Chatham had it. And Burke.

CABANIS: [WILLIAM] I don't understand.

FRANKLIN: It's only the slightest termor at first. You pass it off as a chill, or . . . some indigestion that's left you a bit giddy. Except that you don't recover. And it gets worse. I'm very tired, now, because for months and years I have been straining just to hold steady. Then one day, I happened to look down . . . and saw . . . a long, jagged crack in the ground. Since then I've known that this tremor was sympathetic, passing from the earth itself into my legs, and that all my straining would soon be an effort to prevent a crevass opening . . . and quite futile.

CABANIS: [WILLIAM] *(May lean on chair.)* God help you, Father. Don't say this.

FRANKLIN: To change the world? No. All a man on his little legs can command is his own reason. And reason is a feeble thing next to nature. The nature that's shaking his legs. No, the best that reason can do is look ahead, to try to foresee the motions of nature: given the circumstances of a man, a town, a colony, a country, and knowing how each is bound—by nature—to behave, what things are sure to happen in future years, what will transpire merely "in the nature of things," what forces are going to accumulate that will, because they cannot be reversed or contained, create change in that man, that town, that . . . world.

CABANIS: [WILLIAM] You believe . . . that the colonies must be . . . separate.

FRANKLIN: Will be. Yes.

CABANIS: [WILLIAM] The fact that they have no means . . .

ACT ONE

FRANKLIN: Does not matter. They will accomplish it.

CABANIS: [WILLIAM] And the King.

FRANKLIN: No longer exists. For us. *(Pause.* CABANIS *turns away.)* I know it is hard, William. A reversal of your whole life. But you must make it. Now. I can't control this separation. The fissure is opening, the middle ground you hold is sliding away. It will crumble. You will slip and be swallowed. Please. Come with me.

Silence. Applause. FRANKLIN *and* CABANIS *do not move. Others move forward as they speak.*

TURGOT: Oh ho. And here is where Louis has poured his last millions, and those he never had. Into this crevass.

ROCHE: Doesn't it let out free will, that "in the nature of things."

HELVETIUS: It's the doctrine of the jungle.

MORELLET: Progressive history. It goes against the evolutionary perfectibility of mankind. You are a cynic, Papa.

TURGOT: Papa's never admitted innate goodness, Morellet.

HELVETIUS *speaks aside to* ROCHE.

CABANIS: [WILLIAM] *(Still in character.)* I . . .

TURGOT: No. That's complete. Don't answer.

CABANIS: *(As himself.)* But I want to . . .

ROCHE: *(Clapping.)* Suppertime, suppertime.

MORELLET *cuts swiftly across the stage speaking energetically.* FRANKLIN *will remain sitting by table.*

MORELLET: [*As* CONGRESSMAN] I hereby call to order the thirty-seventh session of the Second Continental Congress of America.

ROCHE: *(Topping* MORELLET *as soon as he begins.)* Don't let him start. He'll debate the revolution start to finish and prove that it couldn't have happened.

MORELLET: [CONGRESSMAN] This morning we will hear . . .

TURGOT: Morellet.

MORELLET: *(As himself.)* But listen, just listen! Here, Papa was meeting with Congress in Philadelphia, and William, right across the river—right across . . .

CABANIS: [WILLIAM] *(Picking up* MORELLET'S *cue, pretends to address New Jersey Assembly.)* Gentlemen: I have taken the liberty to summon you to assembly . . .

MORELLET: . . . called the New Jersey assembly into session.

CABANIS: [WILLIAM] . . . because I want you to know why I have not imitated the royal governors of other colonies—and fled.

MORELLET: Two-thirds of them were ready to string him up.

CABANIS: [WILLIAM] My leaving would certainly have conveyed to the King an irreversible message which I would rather he did not receive. I do not wish the King to believe as he does of other colonies, that New Jersey is . . . in actual rebellion. King George is, as he must, taking necessary steps to put down the rebellion. And I do not enjoy the thought of exposing New Jersey to the . . . measures . . . that must be taken with rebels.

MORELLET: But they were split, nevertheless, they were split.

CABANIS: [WILLIAM] I know that many now speak openly of . . . independence. I know that essays are now appearing in public papers that ridicule the people's fear of such radical action. If, as I hope, you abhor such possibilities, you may do your country great service by declaring yourselves in strong terms, immediately. If, on the other hand, you do not agree with me, if you would rather I fled, then, your course is clear. You have only to tell me so. *(Pause.)* Although I am appointed

ACT ONE

by the King and have sworn my oath to serve him—as you all have too—the day that I no longer speak as your voice to him as well as his to you . . . that day I give up my service, for I have no proper place in this assembly . . . which is a body of free men, chosen by their neighbors, and gathered, with the guidance of their sovereign King, to govern themselves.

Others rise, moved, they group together. FRANKLIN *still sits.* CABANIS *begins to retire, but stops as with an afterthought.*

TURGOT: *(Whispers.)* Masterly.

CABANIS: [WILLIAM] Before I step down I have an announcement to share with you which . . . I don't think you would wish me to delay. I am happy to inform you that your annual pleas have been answered. The King has granted his permission to the assembly of New Jersey to print one hundred thousand pounds.

MORELLET *directs all but* FRANKLIN *in "chorus" of applause, then turns them to respond as members of Congress to his own statements. A roar and applause.* CABANIS *stays downstage.*

MORELLET: [As CONGRESSMAN] Gentlemen of the Congress, I have just been informed that the New Jersey Assembly has appointed a committee to petition King George.

MORELLET *signals uproar from individuals in chorus.* "They can't do that" "No colony can petition separately" "If they get through, why not New York, why not Maryland" "Stop them" "They must be stopped."

During uproar TURGOT *speaks privately to* MORELLET. TURGOT *approaches* CABANIS.

MORELLET: [CONGRESSMAN] *(Announcing* TURGOT.*)* Brigadier General, William Alexander, Lord Stirling.

CABANIS: [WILLIAM] *(To* TURGOT.*)* Stirling. You've no business here. Unless you've resigned your rebel commission.

TURGOT: [*As* STIRLING] You'd have done better to accept one. *(Flings pack, same prop as manuscript used previously, at him.)* Yours?

CABANIS: [WILLIAM] My letters to the King. You're a thief now, as well as a general?

TURGOT: [STIRLING] I think we had better escort you home. You will stay there . . . for the time being.

TURGOT *roughly "escorts"* CABANIS *upstage.* MORELLET *hums a British song off key, perhaps "God Save the King."*

HELVETIUS: *(Stunned.)* Then William went . . . to prison?

FRANKLIN *looks at her, rouses himself, goes to* CABANIS. MORELLET *watches* HELVETIUS *and* FRANKLIN. *Applause and cheers from* TURGOT, ROCHE, MORELLET.

MORELLET: Brava! Brava! Magnificent. But, my god, what a cataclysm.

CABANIS, *disgruntled, turns abruptly from* FRANKLIN *and leaves the stage.*

TURGOT: No. Nonononono. A natural maturation. They were nearly 200 years removed from the presence of a king.

MORELLET: But, Cabanis, what kind of a revolutionary did you turn out to be . . .

MORELLET *sees that* CABANIS *has left.* FRANKLIN *follows* CABANIS.

ROCHE: Come. Fantastique. The playing was inspired. But come, come now to supper.

ROCHE *leaves.* MORLLET *and* TURGOT *are following.*

MORELLET: I say it was monstrous daring.

ACT ONE

TURGOT: Of course. This is true. Still, mon ami, America rebelling is not so revolutionary as France reforming would be.

TURGOT and MORELLET are gone. HELVETIUS remains, looking at the balloon. She is alone for a moment, then ROCHE returns.

ROCHE: *(Quietly.)* Madame.

HELVETIUS: It's all right, Roche. I'll . . . just be a minute.

He watches her uncertainly, she continues to simply look at the balloon. He finally begins to leave, and she speaks again, without looking at him.

HELVETIUS: Do you think . . . If one could just . . . fly up, fly . . . away. It's a silly looking thing, but it . . .

ROCHE: *(Pause.)* Gives hope.

HELVETIUS: Yes. *(Pause.)* What I am going to do.

ROCHE: Answer him.

HELVETIUS: Yes. I must. There's no more time. He'll go away.

ROCHE: *(Pause.)* Why . . . is it so difficult.

HELVETIUS: Because I want him.

END ACT ONE

Act Two

*Late night, after large supper, drinking. Mood will, in general, be more mellow, but just now—*TURGOT *comes storming on stage, from house,* ROCHE *following.*

ROCHE: Come, come, come. Dear Turgot. He didn't mean it. Quiet yourself. Please. Come back. Be peaceful.

TURGOT: *(Ranging up and down.)* Like you, you mean. Like the rest of you . . . sloths.

MORELLET *strolls on, from house, holds upstage, with drink.*

MORELLET: No use, Roche. Better get out of the line of fire. No need to get bruised.

TURGOT: You . . . ! Leave me alone. Get back to your frollic.

MORELLET: *(Walking casually towards them.)* Firing wild now, you see. He won't stop until he's certain he's devastated everyone's evening.

TURGOT: *(Shouting.)* Go away!

MORELLET: Delighted. But I live here.

TURGOT: *(Quietly.)* You do, don't you. While it's convenient, while it's advisable. You can always sniff the convenient table, can't you, and ever-so-deftly pull yourself up to it. With light foot and soaring wit he trips the salon round. Parasite.

MORELLET: By the generosity of Monsieur Helvetius, and the gracious friendship of his widow (whom I worship), for six or so years I have . . .

ROCHE: Do you count me a parasite, Turgot.

TURGOT: You. What do you matter. You sit here with your hands over your eyes and ears simultaneously.

ROCHE *looks at him, turns and walks away upstage.*

MORELLET: You're disgusting. Insufferable. It's all very well to be jealous of our position, especially since Papa has gained the favored-visitor chair, but the scenes you create are no longer tolerable. This jabbing and sniping . . .

TURGOT: Nothing to do with jealousy. I'm simply enraged to see that you have no stomach: talent and intelligence without an ounce of weight. You sway to any favorable wind.

MORELLET: We can't all be obtuse geniuses. *(Pause.)* I am merely a bystander. A connoisseur, if you will, of events. And you must accept that a connoisseur only savors. He never haggles over price, and he never, ever does the dishes.

TURGOT: Coward is the word.

MORELLET: I didn't notice you lining up for an apartment in the Bastille. Who was it stopped contributing articles to Diderot's encyclopedia when it became dangerous? Not I. I tasted it.

TURGOT: *(Pause.)* That had nothing to do with politics. I didn't care to support atheism. Of which you are a prime sample, "Abbe." Glittering with the popular rage.

MORELLET: I suppose you're telling the truth. Because if you *knew* anything about politics you might have been able to keep your position. We'd have been spared the grotesque agonies of your fall. You wouldn't splatter yourself over us every remaining night of your life.

TURGOT: *(Quietly.)* How do you dare. How. You despicable snake. I gave you position. When I became Minister of Finance, you were the first man I called to my side. In the monetary reforms, agricultural projects, governmental restructuring, I trusted you before anyone. What I was trying to do, what desperately needed to be done, was so sweeping, so radical, that faith, trust, dedication had to be absolute. King Louis was with me; he swore to support me unconditionally. And then, when the court pressure against me had become so intense that he was ashamed even to speak with me, I found that you, *you,* were already tripping it gaily in the salon of my successor.

MORELLET: You think I betrayed you. You obtuse fool. I wish I had.

Silence. They stare at each other. ROCHE *comes forward.*

ROCHE: *(Simply, without self-pity.)* I don't think it's right of you to say that I don't matter. I know that I am very quiet and that what I do may not be of great importance in the world, but I believe I have accurately assessed my talents, and chosen to work at the things that are the best that I can do for mankind. I don't think it's right of you to fault me for it.

MORELLET *looks at him.* TURGOT *breaks down crying.* ROCHE *is unmoved. His speeches will be to himself, or to no one.*

TURGOT: Forgive me. God. Forgive me, both of you. I'm mad. I have no more reason. Do you know that it's all falling apart? Our world . . . And there's nothing, nothing I can do.

MORELLET: *(Puts his arm around him.)* Great wounded bear in a cage.

TURGOT: God, god, why did the peak of the world, why so many brilliant men, Montesquieu, Rousseau, Duclos, Voltaire, so much hope for good . . . Why now, just before . . . just before . . . *(Sits down right.)*

ROCHE: Apre moi le deluge. *(Sits by table.)*

MORELLET: The deluge hasn't overtaken us. Not just yet.

CABANIS *appears, from house, considers going elsewhere, slowly enters.*

ACT TWO

TURGOT: If only I had gone more slowly, been more . . . accommodating.

MORELLET: Yes. A pinch of tact might have seasoned several sour dishes. But only at first sitting. Served up the next day, the spartan nourishment would have been spied, and voila, back to the pastries.

ROCHE: *(To no one.)* A man must know not only his strength, but the place of his strength in the cycle of his people. A planter is no use at harvest time.

TURGOT: But there is no money for pastries. My god! There was none then. It is madness. It is as though the more certainly bankruptcy looms, the more wildly the lust for having grows. Bellies swell. There is no more elasticity, no way back, no room even to turn around.

ROCHE: *(Singing.)* Give a girl a pretty ribbon,
  Can you get it back again?
  No. She wants a pretty ring.

CABANIS: Or try now, in the name of economy, to get Morellet to make do with two thimbles of cream.

MORELLET: *(Laughing.)* Ah, here is our future. Come, grant us wisdom, Cabanis. *(To others.)* He will tell us our inspiration lies in Papa's America.

CABANIS: You have to get it back again, Turgot. And Morellet will have to make do. I'm sorry. I shouldn't have said what I did . . . in there, but I . . . we need you. You can direct. And you know the way.

TURGOT: And who will follow. Not even you. You left me to sit at Papa's knee.

MORELLET: Come, Cabanis. Will you, untainted youth, lead your creaking, overstuffed country on the shining path of the West. *(May playfully gesture towards balloon.)*

CABANIS: I'm too young. Theirs was not a rebellion of sons. Grandfathers turned outlaw there. *(Whacks balloon. Looks at them. Turns on heel to leave.)*

TURGOT: And have you seen yet... that France is not America?

MORELLET: Of course he has. He played it out before dinner. He was a Loyalist... in America.

CABANIS: *(Whirls around shouting.)* Leave it alone, Morellet! *(Pause.)* Why not, Turgot, why can't we do what they did?

TURGOT: Because France is old and fat. America was young, struggling. They had no King. Even Papa's generation had never known a King. He was a vision to them, a thing of their imagination, about as substantial as the air in that balloon. So it was simple to make new rules. And to live by them. But you can't turn around an old fat land without great upheaval.

ROCHE: This is a civilization sliding.

TURGOT: Nothing can alter it.

CABANIS: *(Moves toward* TURGOT.*)* Changes are needed, desperately. You know that. As great as those accomplished in America.

TURGOT: But no one *will* change. There is no daring, not one drop of adventure, to be squeezed out of an old man sitting on his pile of coins. He may grunt a bit with discomfort as he feels one or two being snatched from under him. He may expend considerable effort balancing himself when one whole side of his pile slides away. It will depress him; he will groan and be irritable, and blame anyone he can reach with his snarling. But he will never leap to his feet to attack the enemy—never. Not so long as he believes he can preserve one, even one, piece of his pitiful pile by sitting.

CABANIS: But you admit that everything is sliding. What is left for me, for those like me? You make us impotent before we're old. I thought I had the world in my hand. Two brilliant men to show it to me. You're melting while I watch, Turgot. You're flowing away. Why did you lead me, why did you teach me, inspire me, if...

Act Two

TURGOT: I'm tired, Cabanis. Don't look to me. Only catastrophe, only terrible pain will move France to change. And I have known enough of pain already.

Pause. CABANIS *holds, staring at* TURGOT, *then turns and moves swiftly upstage.*

ROCHE: I'm beginning to think that balloon *is* hope. Hope . . . for good, maybe. And just as elusive. Not to be touched . . . by any of us.

MORELLET: Oooolala. A youth too soon moved. He played with Papa and got burned . . .

ROCHE: He has come nearly to worship Papa. That's not safe.

MORELLET: . . . Now he jumps back at Turgot. He's dangling between.

TURGOT: The game did go entirely too far. You should never have insisted on the Congresses.

MORELLET: I couldn't resist. The functioning of their assemblies is amazing, fascinating. Besides, it was only a tag. What business had you to bring up the Privy Council?

TURGOT: I know, I know . . .

ROCHE: Separation of families is the most terrifying thing about war.

MORELLET: Cabanis will want a resolution . . . for William.

ROCHE: The Lippencot question still demands . . . *(Breaks off, thinking.)* It's as though, in one gesture, three warring Kings stood up to say "No. This one love, of these parents for their son is supreme. We honor it. We let it pass between us unharmed."

TURGOT: If Papa did know that William was responsible for Lippencot . . .

CABANIS, *over-hearing, makes for the garden.*

MORELLET: The irony is devastating. *(Pause.)* Cabanis? *(Calling after him.)* Are they finished in there? Have they missed us?

TURGOT: I'll go see. *(He gets up and exits to house.)*

MORELLET: For god's sake, keep it light.

MORELLET *and* ROCHE *shake heads wearily, smile, look at each other.* MORELLET *sits beside* ROCHE.

ROCHE: He'll go see . . . that 'he' and 'she' are not alone.

MORELLET: No harm. If I were master of my life, I should always want to be between her and him. This, perhaps, would not suit Dr. Franklin, who loves to be very close to the lady.

ROCHE: But of course.

MORELLET: Well, then. I would consent to place her between him and me.

ROCHE: What magnaminity.

MORELLET: I think this arrangement fitting for two philosophers who believe in the principle of free trade.

ROCHE: Who do not like exclusive privileges.

MORELLET: Exactly.

ROCHE: But will it satisfy the Doctor.

MORELLET: It should.

ROCHE: Turgot says that she . . .

MORELLET: . . . is moved. Yes, I know.

ROCHE: How would it be for *us* if she said yes.

HELVETIUS *enters from house.*

HELVETIUS: Has Cabanis come this way?

MORELLET: The garden—ah—jungle has him.

ACT TWO   57

HELVETIUS: Ah, then I know where. Would you get the carnival hamper, Roche. We need to play for the gloomy boy. *(She exits to garden.)*

ROCHE Of course.

MORELLET: Success to Turgot. The scarlet bird cannot survive the journey.

ROCHE: You must be wrong about Papa's going.

MORELLET: My dear Roche, just once, look up from your books. I tell you, packing proceeds. Toute de suite.

ROCHE: I don't believe it. So many times, he has sworn he would die here.

MORELLET: I saw more than a hundred crates.

TURGOT *enters on* FRANKLIN'S *arm.*

FRANKLIN: It's nothing, cher ami.

TURGOT: It is not nothing. *(Pause.)* I don't ask you, for the state of your health anymore. You're too stubborn to mind that. I beg you now because . . . in behalf of . . . the lady.

MORELLET: Good god. Get the party props, quick.

ROCHE *exits to house.* FRANKLIN *and* TURGOT *stroll down left.*

FRANKLIN: She set you on?

TURGOT: You know yourself. She has begged you herself.

FRANKLIN: Her begging and her setting you to beg are two different things.

TURGOT: What does it matter if what we ask . . .

FRANKLIN: Did she ask you to speak to me?

TURGOT: You know that she would never impose her troubles . . .

FRANKLIN: Then it's settled. You have no authority.

TURGOT: But as a friend, a dear friend to you both . . .

FRANKLIN: Except as a friend.

TURGOT: She is more troubled than I've ever seen her. She doesn't sleep. You have shattered her tranquillity, brutally. That, my friend, is not friendly. It is not what a caring, loving . . .

He stops, because FRANKLIN *has turned to watch* HELVETIUS *enter from garden. She is consoling a brooding* CABANIS.

TURGOT: If you cared for her you would let her be, you wouldn't feed or allow such agitation.

FRANKLIN: Agitation is not unhealthy, mon ami. Agitation is a sign of uncertainty. And as long as she is uncertain, I will press.

HELVETIUS: Come. Nothing will satisfy this pouting child but to go on. *(She flops onto the floor.)* We must continue the pantomime. Let's bring Franklin to France.

CABANIS *has held at a distance, gloomily.*

MORELLET: That's good, that's right. *(Eagerly, glad to start something.)*

HELVETIUS: *(To* MORELLET, *sotte vocce.)* And for god's sake, keep William out of it.

ROCHE *comes in with basket of costume pieces, props.*

MORELLET: *(To* HELVETIUS) Easy enough. He's tucked away in prison.

ROCHE: We'd just come to us. Voila! The French countryside.

FRANKLIN: Ah, from here on it's pure joy. Once I'd barged my way into your shrine . . .

HELVETIUS: Ooooh, Franklin, don't blaspheme. What goddess receives in muddy petticoats from the dusty floor.

FRANKLIN: The only civilized one I know.

HELVETIUS: That's not the description they'd give me in your Puritan America.

TURGOT: She's always run wild. Her Aunt's salon spoiled her.

MORELLET: But also spared her, mon cher ami, from the raging lusts that prevailed outside. She was a pure enough gem to kindle even the pious Turgot.

HELVETIUS: What do you know—you giddy children.

ROCHE: And mischievous enough to lure him away from the learned conversation.

TURGOT: Enough. That's enough.

ROCHE: A croquet, Abbe Turgot, a little croquet?

MORELLET: Abbe? Oh no. He soon found his true calling was secular. No vows, please, no vows.

CABANIS: That was true. By then, Helvetius . . .

HELVETIUS: Stop this. These two were no more than school boys, and you *(To* CABANIS.*)* weren't even born. So hush.

MORELLET: Ah, yes. By then the dashing Monsieur Helvetius, Apollo incarnate, came sweeping down to envelope her. Alas, poor Turgot.

She laughs, shakes her head.

FRANKLIN: You see, Madame—in your company we are not only pleased with you, but better pleased with one another and with ourselves. You are fine amber. We, poor straws that cling.

HELVETIUS: *(Pause. She rises.)* Come, come, come. This is selfishness. Franklin belonged to France before we knew him.

MORELLET: A music, a music. Let's have the "March of the Insurgents" to accompany the arrival of Franklin on the shores of France.

MORELLET *begins march. All but* CABANIS *go to basket to choose props. Noisy chatter. The pantomimes now take on boisterous, free-for-all quality, and all the characters participate most of the time as they recreate events well known to them.*

FRANKLIN: *(Quietly to* HELVETIUS.) You know where he belongs now.

*Confusion is crystallizing into "*FRANKLIN*" chant.* HELVETIUS *will join* MORELLET, TURGOT, *and* ROCHE.

CABANIS: *(Moving to* HELVETIUS.) What does this have to do with William. He didn't come to France.

HELVETIUS: Come now. Forget that. Enjoy yourself, dear child. We need tonight a little celebration.

Fanfare. "March of the Insurgents." Following lines given by individuals and group as crowd of common Frenchmen. They throw themselves into "play," glad to lift mood; scramble after props or bits of costume to illuminate each character. HELVETIUS *directs. They are grouped loosely, center.* FRANKLIN *sits down right, back to audience.* CABANIS *is not convinced.*

Franklin, Franklin, Franklin. *(Cheers.)* The good man Richard!
He's coming.
Is he here?
That was this morning.
Tonight the word is . . . he has not yet arrived.

Have you seen him?
The father of freedom.
The champion of natural man.
The soul of simplicity.

ACT TWO

And he's rich.
And he tells us how to be rich.
Frugality, perseverance, honest work.
And we'll be rich!

ROCHE: [*As* FRENCHMAN] But we are rich. France is the richest kingdom...

MORELLET: [*As* FRENCHMAN] France is rich. We are not. Ask the Minister of Finance.

TURGOT: *(Mocking himself.)* It's a matter of distribution. Of the flow of capital through...

MORELLET: [*As* FRENCHMAN] Franklin, Franklin, Franklin!

Others pick up chant. Volume increases.

A wise man.
A powerful man.
He's tamed the lightening and torn the sceptre from tyrants.
Franklin, Franklin, Frank...

FRANKLIN: *(Shouts.)* WAaiit.

All quiet.

FRANKLIN: That's not how it was. *(Pause. A fillip of music.)* No. You muddle it all. You jump to the end. To hear you go on, the war had been won. And by me. *(Pause.)* When I debarked I was alone.

CABANIS: *(Moving downstage.)* No. *(Pause.)* Your grandsons were with you. *(Flops in chair down right.)*

FRANKLIN: *(Short laugh.)* Yes. Otherwise I couldn't have stood. *(He hunches, portraying weakness and cold.)* Wind. *(Players create wind sound.)* Everything bleak... Strange stares at us...

ROCHE: But at Nantes...

FRANKLIN: I stumbled, freezing, into a rickety carriage... rattled painful miles...

HELVETIUS *quickly places a chair down right facing* CABANIS, *ushers* FRANKLIN *into it as "carriage". She stands with her back to his as "driver", has a belt for a whip to crack. They "rattle" along.* CABANIS *refuses to play though he's in the carriage.*

ROCHE: But at Nantes...

HELVETIUS *"stops" carriage abruptly.* FRANKLIN *reacts painfully.*

HELVETIUS: [As DRIVER] Pardon me, Monsieur, but... I thought you would like to know. The woods we have come to are creeping with bandits. Only a week ago, Monsieur, several travellers were robbed. On this spot.

FRANKLIN: *(Very weakly.)* I see. *(Pause.)* Well...

HELVETIUS: [DRIVER] And murdered, Monsieur.

FRANKLIN: I see. Well...

HELVETIUS: [DRIVER] Left sprawled in their blood.

FRANKLIN: Well, I thank you for the... information.

HELVETIUS: [DRIVER] No thanks, no thanks, Monsieur. Most honored to oblige.

They resume journey.

ROCHE: But at Nantes...

March begins softly. Also, low, from the others as crowd we hear: "He's coming." "Have you seen him?" "Is he here?"

FRANKLIN: Yes. All right. It's true. At Nantes, it began.

Noise explodes. Other phrases added. "He has no wig. No wig. No wig." TURGOT *and* ROCHE *will help him out of carriage.* MORELLET *is busy over basket.*

TURGOT: [As MONSIEUR PENET] Welcome. A thousand welcomes, great philosopher, to our humble city. Allow me please to introduce myself: Monsieur Penet, entrepreneur extraordinaire. You will please to accompany me. The Friends of America have prepared a great dinner in your honor. (ROCHE *begins his line on "dinner".*) We wish to express our esteem and assure you of our limitless enthusiasm for the cause of freedom.

ROCHE: [*As* MONTAUDOIN] Old friend, I have written a poem celebrating your arrival . . .

FRANKLIN: Ah, Montaudoin. Merchant extraordinaire.

ROCHE: [MONTAUDOIN] I've bought a Dutch clipper . . .

FRANKLIN: I'm a bit tired.

ROCHE: [MONTAUDOIN] Renamed it Benjamin Franklin.

MORELLET: [*As* BEAUMARCHAIS] Excuse moi.

Music dies. All turn to see extravagant figure MORELLET *has put on. Large mustachio, hat, cape.*

MORELLET: [BEAUMARCHAIS] I must pay my respects.

He approaches from upstage grandly, makes sweeping low bow, reaches for FRANKLIN'S *hand, which he kisses loudly.*

MORELLET: [BEAUMARCHAIS] Your servant.

ROCHE: *(Loud whisper.)* It's Beaumarchais.

Others echo "Beaumarchais, Beaumarchais."

FRANKLIN: Delighted, sir. I know your "Figaro" . . .

MORELLET: [BEAUMARCHAIS] Child's play, Monsieur. Here, right here at your feet is where the true soul of a man can become engaged. And I take great pleasure to inform you that by way of my . . . courtly connections, and a bit of . . . ahem . . . back-corridors aaaah activity . . . *(He draws* FRANKLIN *aside and speaks sotte vocce, raising significant words.)* that the *King* of *France* and the *King* of *Spain* will advance *two million livres* to finance my company, masquerading as Hortalez et Cie, but dedicated in deep secret to supplying you with *ships, guns,* and *ammunition.*

TURGOT: *(Quickly changing his "costume".)* Robbery, robbery, robbery. *(Aloud, as* CHAUMONT.*)* Pardon me, pardon me . . . *please.* I cannot comprehend what a practical, simple man like the good doctor could have to gain from a flamboyant, irresponsible, melodramatic . . .

MORELLET: [BEAUMARCHAIS] Irrepressible, irresistable . . .

TURGOT: [CHAUMONT] Play writer.

MORELLET: [BEAUMARCHAIS] I suppose you, Monsieur, have procured two million livres from the King.

TURGOT: [CHAUMONT] Robbery! *(To* FRANKLIN.*)* His dealings are bound to be shady. His motives personal. He was creditor-hounded only last month. While I, Le ray de Chaumont . . . *(Bows, introducing his new character. They applaud.)*

MORELLET: [BEAUMARCHAIS] Pardon me, Monsieur. But what can a bourgeois upstart have to do with the moving of royal courts.

TURGOT: [CHAUMONT] *(Always speaks faster than others can think: a salesman.)* But there it is, there it is. It is not a matter of royal courts. This time it will be the people. And they are already, if they know their hearts, won. It is a simple matter of pro-mo-tion my dear fantastique. The pressing of a few key pedals, the covering of a few essential stops . . .

MORELLET: [BEAUMARCHAIS] You cannot scoff at influence.

TURGOT: [CHAUMONT] There is no need, no need for it. If Voltaire can do without patronage, so can Franklin. The heart of France is Franklin's. It is only for me to reveal it to itself for the blaze to color the sky. *(To* FRANKLIN.*)* I have a factory on the River—fine clay, marvelous clay, going to waste, so I built a ceramics factory. Imported an artist. The best. Giovanni Battisti Nini. *(Tries to draw* CABANIS *in as Nini.* CABANIS *won't budge.)* Italian, of course. Now, if we were to dispatch to

ACT TWO 65

Signoir Nini your image—a sketch would do—and some notes . . . on aspects that are most appealing to the public. Say that fur cap. They've latched on to that.

FRANKLIN: Oh, this. Excuse me. I've been unable to bear a wig . . . the sores on my scalp . . . and . . .

TURGOT: [CHAUMONT] Keep the hat, keep it. Never go without it. Never wear a wig. It's caught on. You've given them a curiosity. Your hat will be the rage. I can predict . . . in two months . . . in two months we can sell . . . ten thousand fur bonnets, for Madame, a la Franklin.

Laughter, applause.

ROCHE: It's the bonnet of Rousseau.

TURGOT: [CHAUMONT] But of course. You have it. Franklin will be the embodiment of Rousseau's ideal. Purity of the primitive. The noble savage.

FRANKLIN: Excuse me; has Rousseau ever met an American savage.

ROCHE: And Voltaire. Pennsylvania. Land of tolerance and virtue. Abundant vineyard of social perfection.

FRANKLIN: Excuse me: has Voltaire ever been to Pennsylvania?

TURGOT: [CHAUMONT] He'll satisfy everyone. A grand combination. The intersection of our great philosophers, of all our aspirations in this one . . . gleaming . . . eagle of liberty.

FRANKLIN: The turkey is a better bird.

TURGOT: [CHAUMONT] This minion of simplicity, the good Quaker.

FRANKLIN: Good god, I'm not Quaker!

TURGOT: [CHAUMONT] *(Pause.)* Now, the means. The means . . . as I was saying, about my ceramics factory. Signoir Nini, in a few day's time, with a proper sketch, can supply us with as many thousands of medallions bearing your image as we can sell. Every Parisian must have one to carry, to wear, to cherish. And plaques. And plates. You'll hang above every mantle. A patron saint. We can put you on snuff boxes, pin holders . . .

FRANKLIN: No. No, nonononono. I must be very quiet.

TURGOT: [CHAUMONT] But of course. You may stay as quiet as quiet as you will. In fact, that's good. The mysterious, silent, humble Quaker.

FRANKLIN: I have come to represent a country your King cannot recognize.

TURGOT: [CHAUMONT] Yes. Mysterious, silent, humble . . .

MORELLET: *(As himself.)* Nonsense. What does that mean.

TURGOT: *(As himself.)* It's true. For Louis even to acknowledge Papa was to risk war with England.

ROCHE: Which we have not survived so well in the recent past.

FRANKLIN: So the first support was secret. And only monetary.

MORELLET: That's true.

FRANKLIN: But my dear friend here opposed even that.

TURGOT: It's true.

FRANKLIN: Had he not been booted out, France would never have lifted an eyebrow for us.

Others are alarmed. Atmosphere tense. CABANIS *is finally interested.*

HELVETIUS: Franklin!

ROCHE: Papa.

TURGOT: I'd do it again. Had I not been booted out, France would be a reformed, prosperous, and healthy country. And America would be free anyway . . . without our help. If not today, twenty years from now.

MORELLET: *(Trying to be light.)* Nonono. No harm. We have

ACT TWO

only to make bread from all the floured wigs at court.

ROCHE: And Morellet must give up cream.

FRANKLIN: *(To* TURGOT.) A somewhat cynical attitude, isn't it?

TURGOT: If I am a cynic, at least I am direct and honest.

FRANKLIN: And I am indirect and somewhat less than honest.

MORELLET: *(Breaking in.)* He is a diplomat, dear Turgot. It is his profession. *(Laughter. A little hesitant.)*

ROCHE: *(Trying to laugh.)* That's it.

FRANKLIN: *(Moving to* TURGOT, *conciliatory.)* The two of us are out of place, and it is the misfortune of us both. His to be born honest in a subtle society; mine, to be subtle in a naive one.

TURGOT: You bled us. Like the infant that bites the breast. We were all but bankrupt when you arrived.

FRANKLIN: That was not for us to know. Or understand. To us you were a great world power . . .

TURGOT: Of course not, of course not. You held the infant privilege of blind selfishness. It was our own stupidity . . .

FRANKLIN: A world power, but without motherly love. You fed us for fear someone else might.

TURGOT: We fed you, nevertheless, and now we sprawl, gasping, because of you.

ROCHE: You exaggerate, Turgot.

TURGOT: I do not exaggerate. Can't you understand that we're bankrupt.

ROCHE: Turgot, the financial report . . .

TURGOT: *(Exploding.)* That report is a hoax. No increase in taxes . . . hah! What is the source of income? Loans, my children, all loans. We haven't a dream of paying them back. The debt, the national deficit, swells geometrically each year. We've forgotten the time when we expected to come out even. And we've squandered our last margin for recovery on this man's revolution. *(He walks away.)*

FRANKLIN: He doesn't exaggerate. And his mind was always the larger. While I counciled one man, he could construct the dynamics of wealth for a nation. No. For France's sake, the minister Turgot was right. And should have prevailed.

ROCHE: *(To no one.)* They said at the moment the fabric was punctured they could see neither earth nor sky.

MORELLET: If you're right, Turgot, it was mean of you to say we haven't the spirit to fly. If you're right, we helped to mount America with the last that we had. That requires the deepest spirit.

TURGOT: Or blindness.

ROCHE: But it was political.

TURGOT: Of course it was political.

FRANKLIN: For King Louis and his ministers, perhaps, but not for the people. They spread out their hearts.

MORELLET: [As BEAUMARCHAIS] *(Trying to return them to pantomime. Puts on his hat.)* Voila. The contention of Monsieur Chaumont: The heart of France. But, do not forget the humble Quaker—quaking in the cold wind of Nantes . . .

ROCHE: The heart of France must be answered. Without that she is nothing. And that heart would give itself to Papa's America. C'est la vie.

TURGOT: [As CHAUMONT] *(Pause. Then decisively assumes character.)* Yes, yesyesyes, my dear humble Quaker. "Mysterious, silent, humble . . . " That's good, that's very good. I have it. You'll stay with me.

FRANKLIN: I must be very quiet.

TURGOT: [CHAUMONT] I have recently purchased a place in the country . . .

FRANKLIN: And I'm not a Quaker.

ACT TWO 69

TURGOT: [CHAUMONT] You'll retire, modestly, from sight, in Passy. Conveniently, it is just off the road to court. You'll retire midway—a ways from Paris, on the way to Versaille. Superb!

ROCHE: Chaumont. Your place in the country is hardly modest. The hotel, estate, and gardens Valentois.

TURGOT: [CHAUMONT] No matter. The good doctor may modestly retire there. He will be my guest. His whole delegation. My personal gift to the cause americaine.

TURGOT *is ushering* FRANKLIN *off.*

MORELLET: [*as* BEAUMARCHAIS] Wait. Wait, my time has come. A message from the King: You may deliver, Monsieur Chaumont, as a gift from the King to the Comtesse de Polignac, one chamber pot. And on its inside base you will emboss, the image of . . . Franklin.

All laugh. ROCHE *tries to top laughter.*

ROCHE: *(Announcing.)* The reception at Versailles.

FRANKLIN: No, nonononono. You're making a mockery. *(Pause.)* You're not remembering the delicacy, the . . . grandeur, the . . . brilliance of mind that France offered me.

MORELLET: You want seriousness, Papa. You want solemn, long, important faces? You forget, excepting the humor of Monsieur Turgot, this is not soggy England. To be admired in France, the most heavy matter must be filliped ever so lightly and caught in the air, so, without missing a single, prancing step. *(Pause.)* Cabanis. You are Louis.

CABANIS: No, I . . .

ROCHE: Come, Cabanis.

He has been pouting. HELVETIUS *directs him to upstage center to be king. He turns his back to the audience.* FRANKLIN *moves to extreme downstage. Others line one side creating corridor. Drum roll. Crowd lines are in hushed whispers.*

He's coming
Is he here?
It's nearly noon.
Quiet. Hush.
How exciting.
Hush.

Pause. FRANKLIN *turns on the first "my god". He begins slow walk up corridor.*

Mon dieu.
He isn't dressed.
He dares come like that.
My god.
He isn't dressed.
They won't admit him.
Mon dieu.
No wig, no sword.
Dressed like a Quaker.
My god.

FRANKLIN *has arrived at spot where* ROCHE *as Royal Chamberlain—in shock and uncertainly—makes move to stop him, may step in front of him, but is cowed by the momentum of* FRANKLIN'S *walk and steps back.* FRANKLIN *sweeps past.* CABANIS *suddenly and swiftly turns to face him.* ROCHE *steps forward, still quivering.*

ROCHE: [*As* ROYAL CHAMBERLAIN] Votre Majeste. Je voudrais vous presenter en cette occasion Docteur Benjamin Franklin, l'ambassadeur d'Amerique.

FRANKLIN *bows.*

HELVETIUS: [*As* QUEEN] *(Giggles.)* L'ambassadeur d'electrique.

CABANIS: [*As* LOUIS] Firmly assure Congress of my friendship.

Act Two

I hope this will be for the good of the two nations.

FRANKLIN: Your Majesty may count on the gratitude of Congress and its faithful observance of the pledge it now takes.

FRANKLIN *bows again, backs away, turns and begins walk.* CABANIS *looks at* HELVETIUS *at his side. "Hush, shhhh, hush" intensifies from others as* FRANKLIN *repasses* ROCHE, *and, no longer capable of being restrained, a cheer breaks out.*

Hurrah!
The good doctor.
Franklin, Franklin, Franklin.
Liberty, liberty, liberty.

FRANKLIN *nearly reaches downstage end of corridor when* CABANIS *whirls again and shouts over noise.*

CABANIS: [LOUIS] Doctor, a moment.

Everything stops. Silence as FRANKLIN *turns back.*

CABANIS: [LOUIS] Where is your son.

FRANKLIN *stares at him. Others are alarmed.* HELVETIUS *tries to intervene.*

MORELLET: Cabanis!

CABANIS: [LOUIS] Silence. I'm the King! *(Pause.)* Where is your son. *(Pause.)* Still in prison?

FRANKLIN: No.

MORELLET: Cabanis!

CABANIS: *(As himself.)* Quiet! This is why we went on, isn't it. Or did you all choose to forget William. *(Pause.)* And Elizabeth. *(Pause.)* Is she with him?

FRANKLIN: No.

CABANIS: [*As* LOUIS] Where is his wife.

TURGOT: *(Breaking in.)* I'll do Franklin now. We can't leave out Voltaire, and Papa's the only one old enough to play him. Come, Papa, stand for Sophocles.

Others bustle to change scene. CABANIS *won't be distracted.*

CABANIS: [LOUIS] *(Shouting.)* Where is his wife.

FRANKLIN: Dead.

CABANIS: [LOUIS] Dead. Why is she dead.

MORELLET: We can't stop before the pirates.

FRANKLIN: She . . . died in New York.

Others try to interrupt. HELVETIUS *is frozen watching* FRANKLIN.

MORELLET: Come, Papa, stand for Voltaire.

TURGOT: He may be too fat for Voltaire.

MORELLET: Well, I want to get to John Paul Jones. I'd like to try a pirate.

TURGOT: Beaumarchais's not bizarre enough for you?

CABANIS: [LOUIS] *(Out of control.)* Alone. Alone. He couldn't even go to her?

FRANKLIN: It was denied. Congress . . . wouldn't allow . . .

HELVETIUS: *(To* FRANKLIN.*)* And you . . . did nothing?

TURGOT: *(Changing the scene.)* Come now, come now. Vive le pantomime. Salute the black days. Painful defeat and uncertainty. Remember Philadelphia.

FRANKLIN: *(Shaken, but trying to get back into game.)* Yes, yes. There you are. Voila.

MORELLET: The French cannot afford to love a loser.

ROCHE: Papa's family, his home, all his possessions—captured by British.

ACT TWO 73

MORELLET: No doubt of it. Yet we hoped . . .

ROCHE: When we knew an American ship had docked . . .

ROCHE *is backing up to get a run.* TURGOT *and* MORELLET *bring* FRANKLIN *to stand with them.*

MORELLET: We fell over ourselves . . .

ROCHE *runs to them as messenger.* TURGOT *and* MORELLET *thrust* FRANKLIN *out to meet him.*

FRANKLIN: Sir. *Is* Philadelphia taken.

ROCHE: [As MESSENGER] Yes, sir.

All droop, and turn to walk away.

ROCHE: [MESSENGER] There's something else, sir. General Burgoyne and his whole army . . . are prisoners of war.

Cheers, music: "The March of the Insurgents".

MORELLET: What. What!

ROCHE: [MESSENGER] Yes. It's true.

TURGOT: Mon dieu.

MORELLET: [As BEAUMARCHAIS] Get me a carriage. I, Beaumarchais, will carry the news to Paris. I, like the wind. *(He mimes galloping on a horse.)* I'll fly, I'll fly, I'll fly . . .

OTHERS TOGETHER: Into a ditch!

MORELLET *mimes collapse, overturning. All laugh.*

ROCHE: He'll carry the news . . . Not on the wing, but . . . in a sling.

MORELLET *gets up with "broken arm".*

TURGOT: Aaah, my silly children. You reduce all to farce. All farce.

CABANIS: [*As* LOUIS] *(Announcing.)* I give you the President. Board of Associated Loyalists.

FRANKLIN *comes to attention.*

ROCHE: What? What's that?

TURGOT: Cabanis, let it alone.

CABANIS: [LOUIS] A leader still. Wasn't he. Wasn't he. Didn't he lead the underground?

FRANKLIN: *(Shouting.)* Yes. Yes. He led raids. He killed. He killed his own people.

CABANIS: [LOUIS] And Lippencot . . .

FRANKLIN: Strung up the rebel while on duty.

TURGOT: *(Trying to smooth over.)* An ordinary casualty. It would never have become an issue if peace hadn't been near.

MORELLET: *(Quickly.)* Washington seized the Asgill boy in order to create an incident.

ROCHE: *(Seconding him quickly.)* An incident. Enemy monarchs pleading for the same life.

CABANIS: [LOUIS] *(Loud, to* FRANKLIN.) Did you know then, that it was William who gave Lippencot his orders?

FRANKLIN: *(Wailing shout.)* I don't know. I don't remember. What does it matter. He has disgraced me from beginning to end. Leave me alone.

HELVETIUS: *(Coming to him, speaking to others.)* Go away now. You're drunk. Go on. Leave us alone. Go to bed. Go away.

Sudden silence.

ROCHE: Madame has spoken.

MORELLET: Get the guitar. Let's go to the garden.

ACT TWO 75

They have started out. TURGOT *stands looking at* FRANKLIN *and* HELVETIUS. *She sits.*

MORELLET: Turgot, come on.

FRANKLIN *has settled down with her.* CABANIS *still stands pouting.*

HELVETIUS: You, too. *(He is not in her sight, but she knows he is there.)* You're a bad boy. Go to bed.

CABANIS *exits.*

FRANKLIN: *(Head in her lap.)* Must I go to bed, too. *(She smiles, smooths his hair.)* May I come to bed? *(She hums and gazes out.)* Sitting in state on one of her hundred couches, she graciously extends her long handsome arm, and with all the dignity of a sultaness says: "Come. Give me your hand. There. I forgive you."

HELVETIUS: *(Pause.)* I forgive you.

FRANKLIN: He was tall and handsome, wasn't he, Monsieur Helvetius.

HELVETIUS: Like no other.

FRANKLIN: And a devil with women.

HELVETIUS: He was very . . . passionate.

FRANKLIN: They were all wild for him.

HELVETIUS: Lust was the fashion then.

FRANKLIN: But he loved only you.

HELVETIUS: After he found me. I think so.

FRANKLIN: *(Pause.)* He was a philosopher.

HELVETIUS: Like you.

FRANKLIN: I should have known him. We've loved the same ideas, the same books, the same . . . woman.

HELVETIUS: But you are strong.

CABANIS *reenters sulkily, stays at one side.*

FRANKLIN: He was not strong?

HELVETIUS: No.

Silence, while they look at each other. They are aware of CABANIS *without looking at him.*

FRANKLIN: You see. You angrily order them, but they cannot bear to leave you.

HELVETIUS: It's you he's come back for. I think we must give him satisfaction, yes? He was so eager to know your William.

FRANKLIN: He pushed too far.

HELVETIUS: Did he. *(Pause.)* You must go further yet.

FRANKLIN: No, I . . .

HELVETIUS: Yes. The war is past. You have made the peace with England. You have won. It is time to give peace to your son.

FRANKLIN: I have no son.

HELVETIUS: You will bring him here. We will love him as we do you. All wounds will heal and be forgotten. You need that . . . to be clean and quiet. Then we can rest here, together . . .

FRANKLIN: Here in paradise.

HELVETIUS: Come, my Franklin. Your soul waits.

FRANKLIN *gets up, walks unsteadily center.* CABANIS *clears throat. They understand that they will play another scene.*

FRANKLIN: I . . . got your letter.

CABANIS: [*As* WILLIAM] Yes. I . . . wrote.

HELVETIUS: *(Quietly.)* He was . . . is your natural child, your

Act Two

child of passion. And think how he has paid. He has had no mother.

CABANIS: [WILLIAM] I hoped we might . . . talk . . .

FRANKLIN: *(To* HELVETIUS.) Why doesn't he say he was wrong.

HELVETIUS: Because he wasn't. You brought him into the world motherless, where he was despised, then taught him to love England, and she gave him power. Love of his mother England made him a man. He couldn't desert her for you.

FRANKLIN: Love of me, emulation of me, made him a man.

HELVETIUS: No. A man must be loved of woman to be a man. He is not you. In trying to be you he would have destroyed himself. You are too strong, too deep, you are gargantuan. No man could become himself through you. And think of the faith he would have needed. You were discarded by the woman you taught him to love, the mother who accepted and rewarded him. And then you betrayed her, questioned her beneficence, conspired, even, to destroy her power. He would have had to give up his new-found self, his strength, his chance for magnificence, to follow you on your wild new way. You asked him to be more than a man. While you are less. You have won. He is destroyed, disgraced, has lost all his power, his possessions, his family. And now he has lost even the mother he loved. Even England finds him a useless embarrassment. He has lost the love he found. He has lost his love.

FRANKLIN: He could have had my love.

HELVETIUS: On condition. On condition that he renounce himself. Love is not a reward. Love is a necessity. It has no conditions. *(Pause.)* You punish him still. You will not forgive. How can you ever hope for peace.

Pause. FRANKLIN *is disturbed but he doesn't move.*

FRANKLIN: He doesn't ask forgiveness.

HELVETIUS: No. He cannot. Anymore than you can. He asks for love.

CABANIS: [WILLIAM] I . . . I want very much to revive . . . to renew . . . our old affection. *(He puts out his hand.)*

FRANKLIN: *(Pause.)* I'm . . . glad. *(Takes his hand.)* That . . . would please me. *(Pause.)* Yes. I would be very pleased.

They are holding each other's arms at arms' length.

CABANIS: [WILLIAM] I only waited . . . not knowing how you felt and . . . thinking there might be some political reasons . . .

FRANKLIN: Yes . . . we couldn't have met before.

CABANIS: [WILLIAM] Both sides . . . keep expecting . . . collusion . . . between us. *(Wanting to laugh.)*

FRANKLIN: *(Does laugh.)* Funny, isn't it. Only we know how far from a worry they are.

CABANIS: [WILLIAM] Yes. *(Pause.)* You . . . you seem well. You are happy here.

FRANKLIN: Yes. Very.

CABANIS: [WILLIAM] Yes. *(Pause.)* You were always good at building families for yourself.

FRANKLIN: I . . . make as much as I can . . . of the day that offers.

CABANIS: [WILLIAM] Never good at gloom.

FRANKLIN: No. *(Pause.)* Have you . . . seen this new balloon. Operates on a very clever principle . . .

CABANIS: [WILLIAM] I want to say to you, that . . . no matter how my . . . actions appear to you, I have always done what I thought right. Cared for my country. If I have been mistaken . . .

FRANKLIN: If. You doubt it?

CABANIS: [WILLIAM] If I have been mistaken, I can't help it. It's a mistake in my judgement then. Because I still can't see it.

ACT TWO

FRANKLIN: You believe you were right.

CABANIS: [WILLIAM] I don't know, Father. I would do the same today.

FRANKLIN: In your position you say that.

CABANIS: [WILLIAM] *(Short laugh.)* Catastrophic, isn't it, yes. I'll be lucky to get a pension out of England. *(Pause.)* If only the other ambassadors had been persuaded to offer reparations to the Loyalists as part of the treaty . . .

FRANKLIN: There was no problem with the others.

CABANIS: [WILLIAM] No . . .

FRANKLIN: They were in favor of reparations . . . initially.

CABANIS: [WILLIAM] But . . .

FRANKLIN: I was opposed.

CABANIS: [WILLIAM] You.

FRANKLIN: I convinced them that the Loyalists deserved no reparations. *(Pause.)* You didn't expect collusion?

CABANIS: [WILLIAM] Then I'm to blame. For everyone . . . If it weren't for me, you wouldn't have robbed the others.

FRANKLIN: My stand was regardless of you.

CABANIS: [WILLIAM] No. Because of me. The opposite, perhaps, of collusion. *(Pause.)* And I wanted . . . so much . . . to be reconciled. My life with you was the joy . . .

FRANKLIN: Nothing could have approached the joy . . . and the triumph . . . If you had stood with me. *(Pause.)* Did you consider that if you succeeded I would be hanged.

CABANIS: [WILLIAM] *(Pause.)* No. You couldn't lose. *(Pause.)* You never lose.

FRANKLIN: Enough. This isn't pleasant. We'll do our best to forget it. *(Pause.)* Now. There are some business matters: I am prepared to cancel your out-standing debts, and to pay you $25,000 for your western land. You need money, and, as as an exile, have no use for the land. I, in turn, will deed it over to your son.

HELVETIUS: Stop it. Stop it. You are finishing with him, not starting new. Here, take his hand. *(She pulls them together, takes their hands.)* Now. Say it, Franklin. *(They look at each other.)* Go ahead. Say it.

FRANKLIN: *(Reciting.)* Come. Give me your hand. There. I forgive you.

From off: "Cock a doodle doo". The three others appear, ROCHE *with coffee tray.*

ROCHE: Bon jour, bon jour, the night has slipped away.

FRANKLIN *drops* CABANIS' *hand.* ROCHE *brings tray to table.*

FRANKLIN: By god. That same noise. From a French rooster.

MORELLET: A cock is a cock the world over . . .

TURGOT: We have received an accurate report.

MORELLET: . . . and will a doodle doo. Will you. Will you?

TURGOT: That no coaches whatever will depart today.

FRANKLIN: Abbe, you should be ashamed.

ROCHE: None whatever. None will depart.

TURGOT: We have the whole of this glorious day to resume . . . our consideration . . . of the progress of man. *(Kisses* HELVETIUS.*)*

HELVETIUS: Good morning, Turgot.

FRANKLIN: *(Purposefully.)* I wonder if you wake me to happiness, Turgot. Come, Madame. *(He takes her hand to lead her aside.)*

MORELLET *and* ROCHE *will bring chairs to the table.*

ACT TWO

TURGOT: Moment, Monsieur, Madame. We must offer up . . . bring forth, the report, findings, conclusions, of the majority . . . the majority herewith gathered, arrived at . . .

MORELLET: What the good minister wants to report is that, having traversed the bowels of Madame's abundant, lain in . . . jungle, it has occurred to us eminent philosophes, one and all, that what we have here is a succulent haven, a nook . . .

ROCHE: No, no, no. A hothouse.

MORELLET: That's it. A hothouse. Thanks to the financial abundance of our late esteemed Monsieur Helvetius, wherein we indulge our tendencies to debate and propagate in bountiful blooming array, multitudes of theories and systems of human life to the greater glory and advancement of our fellow citizens.

ROCHE: Subjects.

HELVETIUS: They're all drunk.

MORELLET: Subjects.

TURGOT: But that essentially . . .

CABANIS: But that essentially we crouch here licking ourselves—academics who rub each other's asses.

MORELLET: Oh, oh, oh. What has become of the young doctor Cabanis?

HELVETIUS: Franklin has not forgiven his William.

MORELLET: Ahhh. His eagle is tainted. The strong man is impure. *(Indicating* FRANKLIN.*)*

FRANKLIN: Such a haven is the only mature civilization I have ever witnessed.

MORELLET: And the pure man is impotent. *(Indicating* TURGOT.*)*

TURGOT: Cabanis sees our superfluity . . . and he is the man that must carry France forward. *(Gesturing grotesquely.)* Into the dawn.

MORELLET: Alas, poor fools.

CABANIS: It's not your fault. *(To* TURGOT, *moved.)* Your work was monumental. The simpering King...

TURGOT: Do not make him small. I held his trust, he supported me against everyone... for a time. I think he would have followed me even down a road that reformed him out of existence.

FRANKLIN: Like any loyal son.

TURGOT *steps upstage with* CABANIS. ROCHE *sits nodding, nearly asleep.* MORELLET *has his head on the table.* FRANKLIN *and* HELVETIUS *stand looking at each other.*

ROCHE: Some men fulfill their ambition and some fail. Either way they must make peace with their pride. And their pain. Each man alone.

FRANKLIN: *(Drawing* HELVETIUS *aside.)* Come, Madame.

HELVETIUS: You're not leaving us. I know...

FRANKLIN: Are you going to marry me.

HELVETIUS: Franklin. I've asked you not to...

FRANKLIN: Come. I have no more time to ask.

HELVETIUS: You aren't going to leave us.

FRANKLIN: Madame Love. Love, love, you would have us all love.

HELVETIUS: And you are Monsieur Pride.

FRANKLIN: I have none with you.

HELVETIUS: But you cannot forgive him.

FRANKLIN: It is nothing remarkable to say that I love you. Everyone loves you.

TURGOT *wanders back to look at them.*

ACT TWO

HELVETIUS: Franklin . . .

FRANKLIN: That grand man there has loved you all his life. He has seen you marry and bury a husband. Still he courts. And you refuse.

HELVETIUS: Please, Franklin.

FRANKLIN: He is sorry now that he brought me here. He begs me to leave you in peace. But I can't. And I won't. Because I know that you love me with a love that is more. I know that you would husband me.

HELVETIUS: So proud you are.

FRANKLIN: Am I wrong.

HELVETIUS: *(Pause. She looks at him.)* Don't go.

FRANKLIN: Ask me to stay as your husband.

HELVETIUS: *(Pause.)* You take too much. Those who love you must lose themselves.

FRANKLIN: I would give what's left of my life.

Others will begin gathering at the table.

HELVETIUS: You said it was paradise here.

FRANKLIN: That's not original with me.

MORELLET: I said that. In fact, I wrote it.

HELVETIUS: It's time to rest, Franklin.

FRANKLIN: Father. It's time to rest, Father.

HELVETIUS: What?

FRANKLIN: Someone else said that . . . William. *(Pause.)* I need to rest. It's time. He said so . . . an age ago. If I could have stopped then . . .

HELVETIUS: If you could have, your America might never have been.

FRANKLIN: "But . . . you said it too: how can I ever hope for peace, if . . . *(Decisively.)* I'm the exhibit, yes? The im-perfectibility of mankind. Monsieur Pride. Voila! *(Pause.)* I don't deserve paradise. I must be driven. *(He is embracing them, kissing cheeks, to* MORELLET.) I've left you my work bench. Nails in the left-hand drawer.

MORELLET: The fool must be driven. What other hope.

All are moved, crying or covering it.

HELVETIUS: You said you would stay if I would . . .

FRANKLIN: Will you?

HELVETIUS: *(Pause.)* Why not otherwise.

FRANKLIN: I have always loved. But you . . . are such a woman as I did not dare to hope lived on this earth. But you do. And I have found you. So, in my small prideful mind, the belief has become rooted that if you . . . if you would . . . have me, I would deserve paradise. And it would be time to rest.

HELVETIUS: Otherwise.

FRANKLIN: Otherwise, however you seduce me with your paradise, I am bound . . . to the rough land that bred me. Now she will pick my bones. She's a clumsy child. Who knows how she will endeavor to break her delicate new balloon. *(He is leaving.)* Her freedom. I must be of use. *(Pause.)* Rough and clumsy, she is. But not yet spoiled. There could be as much beauty nurtured there as I have found here. Who knows? She does not.

He goes. Lights have dimmed to glow on HELVETIUS. *She sings to steady herself, but can only get out snatches. We do hear the last line.*

He begged for god-sake I would be his wife,
Or else I would kill him with sorrow.
So, even to preserve the poor body in life,

I think I must wed him tomorrow, tomorrow.
I think I must . . .

HELVETIUS: Don't leave us, Franklin. Franklin! *(Quietly.)* I love you. Benjamin.

END

PROPERTY LIST

Act One

The model balloon—*wrapped in package*
Decanter with wine
Six glasses
Tray
Manuscript
Chess set
Umbrella

Act Two

Large "prop" basket filled with assorted costume pieces: cape, hats, moustache, belt, wigs, etc.

Coffee service.
Cups for six.

www.ingramcontent.com/pod-product-compliance
Lightning Source LLC
Chambersburg PA
CBHW071731040426
42446CB00011B/2313